THE ENTREPRENEUR MINDSET

The art of making ideas happen

DVL Smith

CONTENTS

WELCOME

Today, entrepreneurialism is mainstream. The changing nature of the world of work means that more people see the value of developing their entrepreneurial skills.

Many now recognise the entrepreneurial route as the best way to achieve financial security and get greater satisfaction from the work they are doing in the world.

More people can see the benefit of taking ownership of their working lives and learning how to turn their ideas into action. They can see the end of the era in which people could expect to get a steady job and build a traditional career. These days are drawing to a close.

These changes are putting the spotlight on the need to cultivate the **Entrepreneur Mindset**.

INTRODUCTION

The Entrepreneur Mindset is one that will allow you to take ideas that you've always wanted to progress and turn them into action.

The focus now is on individuals who recognise that they need to always show up with their A-Game and make things happen. We need people who can cope with the highs and lows of entrepreneurial life and feel comfortable navigating the uncertainty ahead.

Who this book will benefit

The increasing interest in the idea of becoming entrepreneurial means that this book will benefit a wide range of individuals.

The primary audience for this book are those who are considering entering the entrepreneurial world and are looking for guidance on how to get started – how to take forward their idea and start thinking like a business owner.

The book will also help those already running a business secure an extra competitive edge.

It will also be of value to those working on a freelance or contract basis.

The book will also benefit those running good causes and voluntary organisations.

And the book will benefit individuals with a creative idea, hobby or interest that they want to bring alive.

There are also ideas for employees seeking to add that extra spark of entrepreneurial flair to the role they play within their organisation.

So, in sum the book is for people who have a passion to make their ideas happen and wish to acquire the Entrepreneur Mindset.

The outcomes we want to achieve for you

Our aim is to provide the reader with a clear direction of travel, an inspirational vision, a plan for setting goals and the ability to focus on what matters most.

We want to eliminate any beliefs that are holding you back and keeping you in scarcity not abundance mode and give you the mental resilience needed for entrepreneurial life.

We seek to supercharge your energy levels, make you super productive and give you the confidence to take timely and decisive action.

We aim to put clear thinking at the heart of your game, allowing you to build strategic advantage, create simple solutions and make informed business decisions.

We want to encourage you to stand out and be different. This you can do by fully understanding and responding to your customers' needs and adding a creative edge to everything you do.

We want to dramatically amplify your presence and help you become an engaging and influential player in your sector. We will help you build your reputation, tell your story and become a personal brand – one that is totally authentic, reflects your personality and is kept vibrant and relevant.

Our ultimate aim is to help you become a high performance entrepreneur, someone who is confident with their decision-making, enjoys the winner's advantage and who has developed powerful success habits.

We want to encourage you to get out of your comfort zone and unleash your full potential. We want to help you build a courageous mindset that knows no limits.

Steve Jobs said, *'Ideas without action aren't ideas, they're regrets.'* We don't want this to happen to you.

So in this book, we provide you with practical frameworks and techniques to build a resilient Entrepreneur Mindset – one that will ensure your creative ideas come to fruition.

The author's experience

It's entirely legitimate for the reader of a book on the Entrepreneur Mindset to ask about the credentials of the person who is framing different techniques and ideas for being entrepreneurial.

In summary, my experience falls into three categories.

I founded a business consultancy, building it up to have offices in Europe, USA and Asia, eventually selling this business. So I know about the highs and lows of the entrepreneurial journey.

I hold a PhD in Organisational Psychology. And I am a Professor at a university business school. In addition, I am a Fellow of the UK Market Research Society, a Fellow of the Chartered Institute of Marketing and a Fellow of the Institute of Consulting. So I can share the key theories and principles that lie behind entrepreneurial and business success.

I also have extensive experience in mentoring, coaching and undertaking consultancy projects for small businesses owners to help them take their businesses to the next level.

But, most importantly, I'm passionate about sharing my experience to help people turn their ideas into action so they don't have any regrets.

Structure of the book

This book is structured into seven parts, each a key dimension of the Entrepreneur Mindset.

We begin with the importance of setting an overall **Direction** for your venture.

We then look at the mental **Resilience** that will be needed on your entrepreneurial journey.

We then examine the critical importance of taking **Action**.

Following this we examine the role of clear deep **Thinking**.

Then we put the spotlight on the need to be **Different** and creative.

Next we look at the importance of being **Influential**.

All of these fundamental building blocks combine to create the **High Performance** Entrepreneur Mindset.

The seven dimensions of the Entrepreneur Mindset

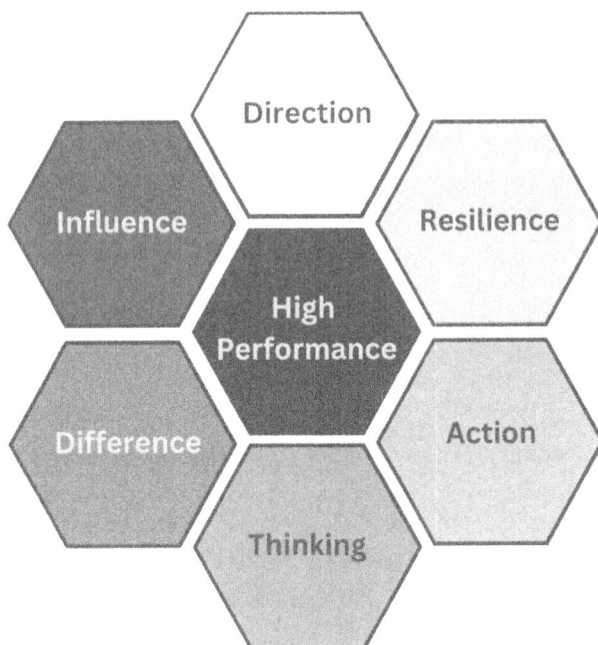

How this book is organised

We have organised the book to provide easy access to practical techniques and actions you can follow – throughout we have provided various summaries and recaps to reinforce key points.

For each Part of the book

We open with an **Overview** of the three chapters within that part.

For each chapter:

We begin with **Highlights** reviewing the main themes.

We outline various **ideas and techniques**.

We then provide **concluding observations**.

We end with **recommended actions**.

We then conclude each **Part** of the book with a **Recap** of the key points made in each of the three chapters.

We follow this format throughout the book.

This structure is designed to provide an accessible text that makes it easy to locate and implement best practice techniques.

Follow-up notes

This book is designed to be a concise practical guide with actions you can take to make your ideas happen.

This is based on the author's extensive knowledge of the relevant research and literature on the topic of what constitutes high performance entrepreneurial behaviour.

However, by design we have not provided detailed references throughout the book. We want to keep it focused on practical advice.

However, for some readers, there may be an interest in following up on certain key references that could be helpful as you progress your entrepreneurial adventure.

So, we have provided in the Notes section a short selection of recommended reading for each Part of the book.

Wishing you every success in making your ideas happen.

PART ONE: SET YOUR DIRECTION
Overview

Good business leaders create a vision, articulate the vision, passionately own the vision, and relentlessly drive it to completion.

Jack Welch

1. Shape your vision

The start point in your journey towards turning ideas into action – making things happen – is to get some sense of your overall direction of travel – the journey ahead. Specifically everything starts with creating a Vision – a picture of what it is you want to achieve in the future.

2. Set motivational goals

Your vision paves the way for setting concrete tangible goals – objectives and milestones – you will follow as you progress towards achieving your vision.

3. Focus with purpose

Then, with your vision in place and with your goals clarified, you need to build the discipline of always acting with purpose and intentionality each day to ensure you achieve your outcomes.

1: SHAPE YOUR VISION
Highlights

Shape a vision for your business

Everything starts with an **idea**: what you want your future to look and feel like.

Your entrepreneurial journey begins with getting clarity around your **direction of travel** – what you want to achieve.

This vision will guide your transformation into being successful - it will be your **North Star.**

Be clear on what you want

Get clear on what you want your entrepreneurial **adventure** to be about.

Step back, take different **perspectives** into account, and get clarity on the vision that works for you.

Imagine your **future self** in your new entrepreneurial role - develop a mental picture of your future business. Get a sense of what this feels like.

Prepare an inspirational vision statement

A simple start point is to write down what it is that you **do want** - and then what it is that you **don't want.**

It is good discipline to create a **vision statement**. This is a written declaration that clarifies the desired long-term outcomes you are seeking to achieve. It sets the inspirational strategic direction for your business - what you want your business to become.

Put this vision statement at the heart of the business you will be **proud** and **passionate** about building.

VISUALISE THE FUTURE: Success starts with developing a clear vision of the future you wish to create for yourself

Shape your vision

A vision is not just a picture of what could be; it is an appeal to our better selves, a call to become something more.

Rosabeth Moss Kanter

Your entrepreneurial journey begins by getting total clarity around what you want your future to look and feel like. It starts with your vision: what you want to achieve and your direction of travel. This will be your North Star guiding your entrepreneurial journey.

And when it comes to your vision make this aspirational and motivational. This will be the compass bearing that steers your entire entrepreneurial venture.

Successful entrepreneurs start with a clear vision of what they want to achieve. They do not just shuffle into existence, almost by default, in a low-key tactical way without any clear defining and aspirational sense of direction.

So, begin with a big picture understanding of what your entrepreneurial journey is all about and build a clear vision – a reference point to which you can constantly refer.

Your vision should reflect what you wish to achieve

Your vision should be inspirational, but anchored in reality

Your vision should be authentic, genuine and reflect who you are

Start with what you want for yourself and others

In crafting your vision, reflect on the fundamental values to which you will adhere to in building your business.

Start by getting clarity around what is important to you and your family in building a business.

Take into account what you want to achieve for yourself and review your responsibilities to family and others.

And get clarity around how running the business will sit alongside your own social and recreational aspirations.

Get clarity around the type of business you wish to create

Be clear on the fundamental nature of the business you want to build. One option is to operate as a lifestyle business. Or you may wish to create an asset you could sell later. Or you may wish to become a serial entrepreneur setting up not just one, but several businesses.

Establish what it is you want and don't want

A sound strategy is as much about knowing what it is you <u>do not</u> enjoy doing as it is about knowing what it is you <u>do</u> enjoy doing.

Clarify how you want to feel in your entrepreneurial role. What are the business activities that will provide meaning and that you enjoy doing?

Why not write down on one side of a page what it is you <u>do want</u> – then on the opposite side, what it is you <u>don't want</u>. This will give you a good sense of how you would like your business to evolve.

Envision your future self

In shaping your vision reflect on your future self. Develop a picture in your mind of you in your future entrepreneurial role.

This will help you programme out any obstacles that may be subconsciously standing in the way of your vision – things that are stopping you thinking big about what you want to achieve.

This technique of constantly visualising a future outcome and acting as if you have already achieved this goal will set you on the right trajectory for success.

Create a vision statement

It is good practice to crystallise your thinking into a 'vision statement'. A vision statement is a written declaration that clarifies the desired long-term outcomes you are seeking to achieve.

This will provide an inspirational strategic direction for your business. It will focus you on what you want your business to become. It needs to motivate you, be inspiring, be memorable and do justice to your values.

Illustration: Brighton My Day

Let's take an example of a young woman based in Brighton. She owns a company called Brighton My Day. The business brings together three core strands of her experience – diet, exercise and wellbeing – into one coordinated offer. She provides a holistic package to those wanting to eat more healthily, exercise regularly and engage in mindfulness.

The vision statement for Brighton My Day could be:

Brighton My Day provides a holistic solution to those seeking the optimum mix of exercise, eating healthily and mindfulness. We stay at the leading edge of sports science, psychology and technology to achieve this. We plan to grow to being the leading provider in the Brighton & Hove area within the next three years.

Refine your vision statement

It is helpful to get feedback and ask others about what they think of your initial attempt at a vision statement. Ask everyone to be honest. Then fine tune your vision statement as appropriate.

In finalising your vision statement it is helpful to ask yourself the following questions:

> Does the statement reflect and do justice to the core values, ethics and principles that I want to follow in setting up a business?

> Is my emerging vision statement providing an inspiration for the future overall direction I want to take my business?

> Does my vision statement take into account my responsibilities to family and friends and other relationships that I need to honour and respect?

> Does the vision statement reflect deep down what I want to achieve for the business and my lifestyle?

> Does the vision statement balance ambitious big thinking whilst acknowledging the realities of what is possible?

> Is my vision statement free from ambiguity and confusion and is it something that will inspire me (and any future employees)?

Give your emerging vision a reality check

Creating a vision will help you think big and ensure you don't act too small and limit your future business horizons.

Your vision needs to be aspirational but grounded in reality. So make sure you have not designed a fantasy vision that quickly evaporates when it comes into contact with the real world.

It is one thing to have a vision about, for example, setting up a successful chain of retail stores in a particular town within a certain time period. But it is unhelpful to set up a vision that says that within one year you want to be bigger than Marks & Spencer!

A vision will help you work on your business

Having a clear sense of direction and staying true to your overall purpose and mission in setting up your business is critical to your success. With this in mind preparing a vision statement will help you work on not just in your business.

It is easy when you are starting a new venture to get carried away with day-to-day events. You can get caught up in lots of admin tasks and activities that deflect you from the fundamental reason why you set up your venture in the first place.

But having a vision statement that you can return to from time to time will keep you focused on the big picture. It will ensure you don't lose direction and drift away from making your ideas happen.

Key actions

✓ Craft a vision that reflects your core values and beliefs – one that provides a mental picture of what you want your business to achieve.

✓ Ensure your vision motivates you, is inspirational and aspirational but grounded in business reality.

✓ Create a succinct and memorable vision statement that crystallises your vision.

→ *Put your vision at the heart of the business you will be proud of and passionate about building.*

2: SET MOTIVATIONAL GOALS
Highlights

Goals focus your effort

Goals are the **platform** for making a success of your business venture.

Setting goals works because they concentrate your thinking and energy - it **focuses** you on outcomes.

Goals help you to **anticipate** any barriers that may lie ahead on your entrepreneurial journey.

Think big when goal setting

It's important to **break free** from any limitations and constraints that are holding you back.

Goals will focus you on where you are now and where you want to go. We want you to think big and **reach for the stars**.

Getting **clarity** around your goals will accelerate your entrepreneurial journey.

Write down your goals

It helps to write down your goals. Keep them clear, precise and **specific** - not woolly and abstract.

Pinning down your goals provides a **tangible focus** for what you want to achieve each day.

Start each day with the **end in mind** - this will give you clarity over how best to achieve your goals.

BEGIN WITH THE END IN MIND: This is one of Stephen R Covey's habits of highly effective people

Set motivational goals

Setting goals helps bring your future into your present and the present is the only time we can take action.
Zig Ziglar

With your vision in place the next step is to set yourself goals. Individuals who set themselves goals tend to achieve better outcomes than those who do not go through this process. Setting goals will motivate you and focus you on where you are now and where you want to go.

Goal setting works because it focuses on an outcome and concentrates your thinking and energy around these goals. This helps you to anticipate and overcome any obstacles that may lie ahead. Goals help you maintain momentum.

Setting goals helps to drive success

Set goals that are aspirational and motivational

The act of writing down goals is powerful

Set grounded motivational goals

In setting your goals it's important to think BIG. Set yourself goals that are motivational and reflect the vision you have created.

Break free from any limitations and constraints that are holding you back.

But avoid setting goals that are not grounded in reality.

A start point for goalsetting is to ask yourself where you are now – then to review where you want to be in say three, then six, months' time.

Commit to writing down your goals

There are no hard and fast rules here. But we would recommend writing down your goals. This is because the physical act of writing crystallises your thinking and acts as a prompt to action. It also creates a measurement yardstick. Tony Robbins reminds us that, *'Setting goals is the first step in turning the invisible into the visible.'*

A high proportion of successful entrepreneurs report writing down their goals in some kind of journal to which they regularly refer.

Think about where your goals will be displayed and how you will refer to them.

Prepare a goal statement

It's helpful to prepare a formal goal statement. Ensure your goals are written in clear, simple unambiguous terms.

For example, the following goal lacks precision and clarity:

> *I plan to improve customer service.*

In contrast the following version of this goal is clear and actionable:

> *My goal is to increase customer satisfaction levels from 55% to 95% within the next three months.*

Don't craft goals around a complex or abstract idea, such as 'be more creative'. This does not give you a tangible concrete focus for how you will achieve this.

The way to tackle a complex goal is to chunk it down into smaller sized goals that are more practical and achievable.

For example, split the uber goal of 'being more creative with our marketing' into tangible activities such as 'improve the creativity of our website'. Then set the goal of 'improving the proportion of visitors to the homepage clicking through to buy a product'.

Illustration: English Country Gardens

Let's take the example of an independent garden landscaping start-up where the vision is to be the leading landscape gardener in the local area.

An example of a 'vague' goal for the business is:

○ To increase revenue and profit and provide customers with a quality service.

In contrast, a more focused and powerful set of goals for this landscape business would be:

○ To increase revenue to £250K by the end of the next financial year and operate with a gross margin of 50%.

○ Generate a personal disposable income of £50K per annum.

○ To be voted the Landscape Gardener of the Year in the local regional competition and to build a reputation for transforming garden space into an outside experience that will delight customers.

Assess your goal setting process

Below we provide a checklist of questions to ask yourself in evaluating your goal statement:

○ Does your goal statement reflect where you want to take the business in the future?

○ Are your goals aspirational, motivational and challenging, but at the same time achievable and realistic?

○ Are the goals written in a clear easy-to-understand way that is practical and actionable?

○ Are your goals measurable – allowing you to hold yourself accountable in delivering these goals?

○ Have you factored into your goal setting how they may evolve over time?

○   What 'price' am I prepared to pay to achieve my goals?

Ask a 'critical friend' or trusted colleague to provide you with honest feedback on the clarity of your goals.

(A critical friend is someone who is encouraging and supportive, but who also provides honest and often candid feedback that may be uncomfortable or difficult to hear.)

Measure your progress in achieving your goals

Take personal responsibility – accountability – for measuring, in a concrete way, your progress in achieving your goals. Use your goals to help you focus and boost your productivity.

For instance, if you set yourself the goal of becoming more knowledgeable about Facebook advertising, you could note down three specific webinars that you need to watch. Then keep a record of whether you did watch, and learn from, these webinars.

Be prepared to adapt your goals and be flexible

It's legitimate to be pragmatic and to adjust goals on a rolling basis to suit different scenarios. There's no point in having goals that have become an unrealistic straitjacket that hinders your motivation and progress.

However, you don't want to set a goal in the morning and flippantly change it in the afternoon for no good reason!

One approach is to periodically review the appropriateness of your business goals in light of changing circumstances and deciding – possibly in discussion with a trusted colleague – whether or not any adjustments need to be made.

Writing down your goals helps deliver outcomes

Most people embarking on a new initiative will have some sense of the goals they wish to achieve. But we are learning that those individuals who take the specific step of creating precise concrete goals, and then writing them down in some form of journal, do better in achieving these goals than those who only set vague, loose goals.

So we would commend the discipline of formally writing down your goals: the physical act of writing down your goals helps them materialise.

Key actions

✓ Set big goals that will motivate and inspire you but ensure they are grounded in reality.

✓ Set goals around activities that drive successful outcomes for your business.

✓ Write down your goals – the act of writing will crystallise your thinking.

→ *Start each day with the end in mind with a clear picture of the goals – outcomes – you want to achieve.*

13

3: FOCUS WITH PURPOSE
Highlights

Take ownership

The concept of **acting with purpose** and intentionality lies at the heart of the Entrepreneur Mindset. It's about considered thinking - not just shuffling into things by default on autopilot.

Always **act with intention.** Take ownership - rather than leaving things to others.

Take **personal responsibility** for making things happen - it's all down to you.

Steer your own course

Successful entrepreneurs see themselves as the **Captain of the ship** - they chart their course and don't meander around aimlessly.

They **drive their own agenda** and don't let others distract them. What they want to achieve is always top of mind.

Entrepreneurs take control of their **own destiny**. They make their own luck.

Prioritise big ticket issues

Entrepreneurs are very **deliberative** and purposeful about how they prioritise and utilise their time.

They always work on **what matters most.**

Acting with purpose is as much about knowing what it is you should <u>not</u> be doing, as it is about **knowing what you should be doing.**

ASK YOURSELF THROUGH THE DAY: Is what I'm about to do going to move me towards my goals and achieve the outcome I want to achieve?

Focus with purpose

The successful warrior is the average man but with a laser-like focus.

Bruce Lee

Warren Buffett and Bill Gates, when independently asked what was the key to their success, spontaneously said that this was their ability to focus (and act) on what matters most.

So focusing with purpose lies at the heart of the Entrepreneur Mindset. It's important to retain a clear sense of your direction of travel – then always acting with purpose and intention to achieve key outcomes. Do not just shuffle into things by default on autopilot.

Act with purpose – be clear on what you want to achieve

Focus on what will deliver the best outcome

Ruthlessly protect your time and energy

Develop a clear sense of purpose – then act with intention

Successful entrepreneurs are totally focused on what will deliver success. Everything they do has a clear intentionality.

They constantly ask themselves whether what they are about to do is going to help them achieve their goals and desired outcomes.

Many high performers have an early morning habit of envisaging the outcomes they wish to achieve that day. They start by focusing on the end in mind.

Take ownership

Take ownership and personal responsibility for your business – rather than assuming that others will somehow sort things out.

It is about having that overall 'executive vision' – seeing the big picture view of what is happening and always knowing when <u>you</u> need to act with intentionality.

Recognise that in your entrepreneurial role it is <u>you</u> who will need to make things happen. (Remember, as an entrepreneur, 'it is always your fault!')

Drive your own agenda

Successful people drive their own agenda. They don't let other people do this for them.

It has been said that, *'If you don't have an agenda somebody will give you one!'*

Ruthlessly manage your time

Maximise the use of your most precious entrepreneurial commodity – time. Acting with purpose and intentionality is about making a conscious choice about what to do with your time. Know how to own your day and protect your accessibility.

Don't meander around aimlessly – use your time efficiently to drive your agenda. Don't let others deflect or distract you.

Always prioritise

Prioritise issues that are important in moving the needle for your business ahead of other less critical activities. This is common sense but not always common practice!

Warren Buffett introduced the idea of 'pro-prioritising'. Essentially this is based on the idea of starting with an initial list of goals – maybe up to 25, and then circling the top five.

This allowed Buffett to focus intensively on his 'circled goals', those he deemed to be the most valuable and beneficial – and therefore the most deserving of his time and efforts.

The Yes & No technique

It is a helpful discipline to actually write down at the start of the week reminders of what you will say _yes_ to and to what you will say _no_.

Peter Drucker said, '*Nothing is less productive than to make more efficient what should not be done at all'*.

Get control of your inbox

Get critical stuff done before you hit the day's emails and start checking social media.

Avoid crazy makers, time thieves and energy robbers

Minimise the time you spend with individuals who will waste your time and sap your energy.

Spend time around kindred spirits, those who will boost your energy, enthusiasm and focus.

Make sure you can see your actions in the calendar

One technique to encourage purposeful action is to ensure that each idea you are scheduling for action is logged into your calendar for a particular day. This linking of a proposed action to a point in time in your diary is more effective than simply putting it on a never-ending 'things to do' list.

Progress on different fronts but with focus

Those with the Entrepreneur Mindset know the importance of being able to simultaneously progress many different initiatives. But they don't hop around from one activity to another in a loose way. They fully concentrate on one key outcome at a time before moving on to the next task.

So, they will be 'multitasking', but they will work on each activity with 100% concentration.

Focus on outcomes not activities

See your day as being about achieving a number of major outcomes that lead towards you achieving your business goals. Do not just see the day as a series of activities. Be effective not just busy.

Let's take an example. An <u>activity</u> would be something like reorganising the filing system – it needs to be done but it won't directly drive your business success.

In contrast, an <u>outcome</u> could be writing a blog post to promote your business, or designing a marketing campaign or contacting 25 potential customers.

Performance experts suggest that you should be spending at least 70% of your working day focusing on key outcomes – things that move the needle – and only 30% on other tasks needed to support you in running your business.

Create do not just consume social media

Don't just be a passive consumer – a recipient – of social media: take part. Be a producer and creator.

Spend some time writing creative and impactful social media posts and blogs that will build your business and brand, rather than just consuming endless content.

Set up a purpose journal

It's helpful to set up some form of 'purpose journal' to help you honestly self-monitor your performance in staying focused.

Keeping a journal is a great way of cultivating the habit of always acting with purpose and intentionality. It will help you stay focused on productive outcomes and stop you from drifting off into periods of aimlessly just being busy.

Why not score yourself at the end of each day. Give yourself a 10 for 'What I did today moved me towards my goals.' And a 1 for 'I got side-tracked and did not make progress towards my goals.'

Own your day with purpose

The notion of always asking yourself whether you are acting with purpose and intentionality, rather than aimlessly drifting off to do busy, but less effective, tasks is crucial to building the Entrepreneur Mindset.

It is vital that you don't just sleepwalk through the day responding in a knee-jerk way to 'events' and crazy makers – the time and energy robbers. Instead ensure that you are always driving forward your own agenda. This lies at the heart of turning ideas into action and making things happen.

Develop the discipline of regularly asking yourself throughout the day: 'Is what I am about to do going to help me achieve my vision and goals?'

Key actions

✓ Stay focused on what matters most. Ensure what you are about to do next will help you achieve your purpose – your intended outcomes.

✓ Be ruthless in how you deal with attempts to rob you of your most valuable asset – your time.

✓ Honestly monitor your performance in always acting with purpose and intentionality.

→ *Always act with purpose and intentionality.*

19

PART ONE: SET YOUR DIRECTION
Recap

Shape your vision

We started with the idea of making your vision your North Star. This will ensure that, notwithstanding the day-to-day pressures, you have a clear picture of your ultimate aim. It was Nelson Mandela's vision of a South Africa free from apartheid that sustained him through his 27-year imprisonment.

Set motivational goals

We then stressed the importance of goal setting. We know that Bill Gates is committed to goal setting using his OKR method. The O stands for first setting Objectives. These should be significant, action orientated and aspirational. Gates then identifies the key results (KR) – targets to be achieved in meeting these objectives.

For example, let's say that you are a dog walker. You could set the 'objective' of becoming the top dog walker in your city. And to accomplish this the 'key result' might be to secure ten new clients by the end of a specific time period. So you have an objective and a key result.

Focus with purpose

And finally we recommend asking yourself whether or not a task or activity you are considering undertaking is likely to achieve your ultimate purpose.

Ingvar Kamprad, the founder of IKEA, was rather obsessive about always acting with purpose and intentionality. Apparently he used to ask himself every ten minutes a question along the lines of, 'Is what I am about to do going to help me build the IKEA empire?'

PART TWO: CULTIVATE MENTAL RESILIENCE
Overview

I can be changed by what happens to me.
But I refuse to be reduced by it.

Maya Angelou

4. Build positive beliefs

In the opening chapter of the next part of the book, we look at ensuring you are not held back by any negative or limiting beliefs. We focus on acquiring the mindset needed to unleash your true potential. Interestingly, even the most successful entrepreneurs report, at the beginning of their journey, not feeling worthy and deserving of achieving their goals. They had to work at building positive self-belief.

5. Think abundance

In this chapter we look at feeling comfortable around wealth and money. This is about cultivating the abundance, not scarcity, mindset. It all starts with building the belief that there is nothing wrong with acquiring wealth. You may wish to use this wealth to reinvest in your business, support others or channel into various good causes.

6. Overcome adversity

In this chapter, we look at overcoming adversity and showing tenacity in the face of any setbacks. For entrepreneurs, the highs are higher, but the lows are lower. So, building techniques to help you stay centred and balanced during your entrepreneurial journey is vital. We show you how to bounce back from setbacks and stay focused on your vision and goals so as to ensure your ideas happen.

4: BUILD POSITIVE BELIEFS
Highlights

Don't play small

Many individuals are held back **by limiting subconscious beliefs** that get in the way of maximising their true potential.

You need to **think big**. Don't let negative beliefs stop you from achieving success.

Break the chain

Clear away any mental clutter that may have accumulated on your journey through education and your career that blocks your belief in yourself.

Thoughts can be managed - don't let any negativity block your progress towards entrepreneurial freedom.

Be disciplined in **breaking out of any destructive beliefs** lurking in your mind.

Programme your mind for success

Put limiting beliefs in their place. Envisage what success would look like if you liberated yourself from the straitjacket of limiting beliefs. Start to look on the bright side of life!

Why not write down an acquired limiting belief and why you believe it to be true? Establish if this belief is simply 'a thought' rather than being grounded in reality. Now **reframe your thoughts** to build a winning Entrepreneur Mindset.

BUDDHA: Your mind is a powerful thing. When you fill it with positive thoughts, your life will start to change

Build positive beliefs

Our deepest fear is not that we are inadequate. Our deepest fear is that we are powerful beyond measure… Your playing small does not serve the world.

Marianne Williamson

We know that subconscious beliefs hold people back from maximising their true potential.

So, clear away any clutter and baggage you may have accumulated on your journey through school or early working life that is blocking you having total belief in yourself.

Remember, a thought is just that – it does not necessarily reflect any kind of reality.

Build positive belief structures

Identify limiting beliefs that block entrepreneurial success

Avoid sabotaging your own efforts

Address belief structures limiting your potential

Don't let limiting beliefs about what is possible stop you from achieving success. You need to think big and believe in your ability to create positive outcomes.

Syd Banks, the Scottish philosopher, reminds us that *'You are only one thought away from happiness and one thought away from sadness. The secret lies in thought.'*

Eliminate any nagging limiting or destructive beliefs lurking in your head that are getting in the way of you taking that next step towards entrepreneurial success. You need to believe in your ability to create a positive outcome for your business.

Reframe any negativity

Start by focusing on any specific negative beliefs or barriers that are getting in the way of you making a success of your entrepreneurial journey.

Why not create a checklist of limiting beliefs that may have emanated from childhood, education, or early work experiences. For each, write down why you believe each limiting belief to be 'true'.

Next, reflect on the veracity, substance and extent to which this belief is simply your thinking, rather than being grounded in reality.

Then envisage what success would look like if you could liberate yourself from the straitjacket of what is simply a limiting belief – a 'thought' without substance. This reframing of your thoughts will help you build a robust mindset.

For example, let's say that you carry the deep-seated belief that you are incapable of understanding complex online digital marketing processes. Here – however true this seems to you – we are entreating you to explicitly challenge this belief, and then visualise what success would look like without this mental block limiting your progress. Say to yourself *'Just how difficult can it be – it's just a matter of figuring it out.'*

Deploy belief-busting techniques

It is said that self-doubt kills more dreams than failure ever did. So, building on the above, we now outline below some techniques with which you may wish to experiment in order to eliminate limiting beliefs that are holding you back.

Visualisation

As we touched on above, visualising success is a powerful weapon. It is a technique that successful sports men and women deploy. Jack Nicklaus, one of the world's greatest golfers, said, *'I never hit a shot, even in practice, without having a very sharp in-focus picture of it (what I am seeking to achieve) in my head.'*

Verbal affirmations

A further idea is to accompany the success you have visualised with a *verbal* affirmation. Picture a successful outcome and say 'Yes I can do this'. This is in contrast to thinking negatively and adopting a 'No I can't do this' mindset.

Delete that programme

Another technique is to mentally delete any negative 'programming' and replace this with a new version of yourself – one in which limiting beliefs have been put in their place.

Specifically, envisage events as being part of a 'movie.' Then recall a negative scenario within the movie. Then press a mental *delete* button on this negative event – and replace it with a more positive 'movie' showing how you are successfully dealing with this situation.

Role play

Another way of overcoming limiting beliefs is to role play. For example, David Bowie, who initially was a reluctant performer, overcame his natural shyness by taking on the role of his alter ego – Ziggy Stardust.

And if you are an aspiring footballer who believes he/she can't score a penalty, why not role play being Pele – one of the world's greatest ever footballers – and assume his identity as you practice taking penalties!

Eliminate any self-sabotaging behaviours

Some business owners find ways of snatching disaster from the jaws of victory! They will sabotage their own efforts.

For example, if a project report needs just one extra hour to get it right, the self-sabotaging business owner will convince themselves they don't have a spare hour. They will submit the report without the final checks and fail. Why, you might ask?

Well, this business owner may be frightened of failing. He lacks the confidence to submit his best possible work. By not doing those final checks, if the client is not happy with the overall report, he can now fall back on the excuse that the deadline was unreasonable, rather than accepting he has 'failed'.

In contrast, the successful entrepreneur will not self-sabotage the project – they will prioritise and ensure they carve out the extra hour needed to get the report just right.

Another reason for self-sabotaging behaviour is a fear of 'success', not failure. In this scenario people worry about whether outstanding success will catapult them into a new high-profile world that may bring intimidating unknowns and uncertainties.

Therefore, you need to recognise these self-sabotaging patterns of behaviour, call them out and eliminate this kind of thinking from your mindset.

Tackle imposter syndrome

In breaking out of limiting beliefs you may also need to tackle imposter syndrome. Amazingly, even great novelists, artists and performers who are at the absolute top of their game sometimes suffer from a feeling that they don't deserve to be successful.

They believe that one day someone is going to tap them on the shoulder and accuse them of being an imposter.

Apparently, Peter Hall – even though he was the celebrated highly successful Director of the National Theatre – harboured the anxiety that he would one day get that 'What do you know about drama?' tap on the shoulder.

So, you need to build the mental strength to overcome any negative voices in your head questioning your capability and your right to be running a successful business.

Reinforce positive thinking with action

Fostering a positive thinking mindset is powerful. But there is more to it than this. This positivity needs to be underpinned by taking action to encourage positive outcomes.

So your positive thinking around the elimination of positive beliefs is the start point. But it will be reinforced if you constantly take small, constructive actions that move you in the direction of achieving your outcomes.

A concrete example here would be to underpin your emerging belief that you are worthy of greater reward by taking the action of increasing your charge out rate, and then confidently telling prospective clients that this is the new rate.

Envisage a future history

One way of cultivating positive and constructive belief structures is the future histories technique. This could help you acquire a positive mindset and a set of supporting behaviours.

Here you need to paint a visual picture in your mind – a future history – of what you are trying to achieve.

This positive mental picture will galvanise energy around the goals that you have set for yourself – the visual outcome on which you are focusing. This energy will then ignite positive triggers that will prompt you to take the action needed.

Illustration: I am the greatest

Muhammad Ali, even <u>before</u> he was the heavyweight champion of the world always used to say, 'I am' not 'I will be the greatest'. His use of language was designed specifically to boost his confidence.

Ali would paint a vivid picture in his head of what he would feel like once he had achieved his ambition of becoming the heavyweight champion of the world.

It wasn't through arrogance he said, '<u>I am</u> the greatest'. It was part of the psychology of using positive language to keep a mental picture alive in his head of what he wanted to achieve in the future.

This technique helped him feel – almost taste – what it would be like when he became the heavyweight champion of the world.

Ali said, *'It's the repetition of affirmations that leads to belief. And once that belief becomes a deep conviction things begin to happen.'*

Build your confidence through enhanced competence

Overcoming limiting beliefs goes beyond the management of thought processes and starting to take reinforcing action. It is also about acquiring the skills and competences to overcome a limitation (as opposed to believing that this is an impossible skill to acquire).

Interestingly, at the heart of being confident is not an overwhelming sense that you can do anything – that you are some kind of superhero. It's a belief that, even though you can't do what is required now, you have the resolve to find out how to build this capability into the future.

It is helpful to think of confidence as being a genuine belief that you will be able to figure things out, rather than it being a mysterious super power.

So when a challenge or obstacle surfaces, always believe that you can find the time, resources and acquire the skills to overcome this. You might not be able to do something straightaway. But it is important to cultivate a deep-seated belief that you will always eventually be able to master the skills needed to solve the problem.

> Think of this as the *Confidence Competence Virtuous Circle.* You invest time and effort in building competence to overcome a limitation that is currently perceived as a barrier. Success then gives you the confidence to start tackling a similar task next time with greater belief and competence. And so, you create a virtuous circle of ever improving levels of confidence and competence.

Be clear on your areas of mastery

In developing competency identify those areas that you must personally master, as opposed to those areas where it would be more appropriate to delegate or subcontract those skills.

Studies of prolific high performers tell us that they are very clear on areas they are going to cultivate, master and excel in, as opposed to areas they just need basic competence.

Sustain your self-belief with positive language

We have introduced the idea of 'verbal affirmation': using positive language to help stay focused on the desired outcome.

Many will be familiar with individuals who tend to frame things 'away from' the positive. Thus, here the question: 'How are you today?' only elicits the response 'Not bad!'

This is in contrast to those who always use language that 'accentuates the positive'. For these individuals their answer to our question 'how are you?' would be 'I feel fantastic!'

The power of building positive beliefs

Self-sabotaging or undercutting one's true potential – snatching disaster from the jaws of victory – is a major challenge for many people.

So there is immense power in learning how to constructively manage your thoughts. Why play small? This is not the way to make things happen.

It seems staggering that people – whether it be through fear of failure, or fear of what success might bring – almost deliberately underachieve and do not realise their true potential.

The good news though is that there are simple and effective techniques on hand to help build a positive mindset. You must learn to 'delete that negative programme'. Do not let self-sabotage undercut your potential.

Key actions

✓ Identify and challenge any subconscious limiting beliefs that undermine the achievement of your vision and business goals.

✓ Spend time cultivating techniques that will strengthen your mindset.

✓ Build your competence. This will take you to the next level of confidence, thus, creating a virtuous circle of success.

→ *Put limiting beliefs in their place. Delete any negative programming and replace with a positive version.*

5: THINK ABUNDANCE
Highlights

Attract wealth – don't repel it

Don't be diffident and anxious around money - make sure you receive your true worth. Attract wealth towards you and your business.

Start to feel comfortable around the idea of **acquiring and enjoying wealth**.

Feel good around wealth and money - **you're worth it!**

Envisage abundance

Get into abundance mode **-** start seeing everything as being attainable and possible. Think abundance - **here comes the sun!**

Entrepreneurs get **beyond scarcity mode** - where everything is seen to be unattainable or scarce.

Eliminate scarcity thinking that blocks **money flowing to you** and plays on negative beliefs buried in the subconscious. This undercuts your entrepreneurial potential.

Reframe for wealth

Shifting limiting beliefs around wealth should be a priority. Start by trying the **Future Wealth Histories** technique.

Think as if what you want to achieve has already happened. Hold this mental picture in your mind - what does this look and feel like?

This abundance version of events will help to **reverse negative beliefs** you may have about wealth and money.

SUZE ORMAN: 'Abundance is about being rich with or without money'

Think abundance

Abundance is not something we acquire. It is something we tune into.

Wayne Dyer

Your relationship with wealth and money should not be a struggle, but a natural process about acquiring what your feel you need.

Build an abundance not scarcity mindset when it comes to how you think about money. Start attracting wealth – don't repel it.

Kick out unhelpful beliefs about money that are hidden away in the subconscious mind that can make it difficult to build a healthy relationship with money.

These blocks around the concept of generating wealth and abundance could be based on early life experiences. But whatever the reason they can lead to living in scarcity mode.

But, if you are a business owner, self-employed or a freelancer, it is critical that you think in abundance mode. Begin to attract wealth towards you and your business, rather than being diffident and anxious and not receiving your true worth.

Build an abundance not scarcity mindset

Eliminate blockages to thinking positively about wealth

'Act as if...' build a healthy relationship with money

Cultivate an abundance not scarcity mindset

As an entrepreneur, see the world through an abundance lens where everything is attainable. Cultivate a wealth mindset that will deliver your vision and goals: envisage abundance.

A scarcity mindset can block money flowing to you. It undercuts your entrepreneurial journey. It plays on negative thoughts, beliefs and mantras buried deep in the subconscious. It blocks and sabotages progress towards building a successful business. So, it is important to think abundance.

Get clarity around your wealth goals

Let's look at a technique for shifting deep-seated limiting beliefs around money and removing any blockages to abundance. Start by taking time out to reflect on the wealth goals you wish to achieve.

Ask yourself questions about what you want your business and working life to look like. Are you building a business to have a steady, ongoing income? Or do you want to build a big saleable asset?

Building on this, clarify what revenue you want to be achieving, the level of profit you are seeking and what this means for your desired personal income and lifestyle.

This clarification of, and reflection around, your wealth goals will provide context and perspective to help build your confidence around money.

Become congruent with money

Now, building on your reflections about your desired lifestyle, undertake a self-assessment exercise on your attitude towards abundance. Assess where you are on the following statements.

I feel wealthy
Thinking of money gives me joy
My life is filled with abundance
My attitude towards money is always positive
I enjoy prosperity
I naturally invite good fortune
Acquiring money is good
I rarely get anxious about money
I feel that money will come my way

Score yourself on each statement using a scale where 10 means 'this statement totally describes me as a person', and 1 means that 'it does not describe me at all'.

This informal assessment is designed to encourage you to reflect on where you are in your journey towards having a healthy mental attitude towards money.

Use this exercise as a way of helping you pinpoint whether there are any specific blockages lurking in your subconscious making it difficult for you to achieve your wealth goals.

Reframe to shift limiting beliefs around money

Recognise that your initial thoughts are only one way of thinking about money: you can reframe – rethink your relationship with money.

Identify a specific issue where you sense there is diffidence, anxiety or underachievement around wealth.

Then reframe this thought to get into an abundance register and reverse negative beliefs about money.

Think Future Wealth Histories

The Future Histories technique we discussed earlier used by Muhammad Ali can be adapted to future *wealth* histories.

Mentally picture in your mind what you want to achieve – what does this look and feel like? This abundance version of events will help to reverse any negative beliefs you may have about wealth and money.

So let's say you have come to believe that your business does not deserve to receive funding from a grant awarding government body.

Well here replace this negative thinking with a positive reframing of events. Why not picture yourself in the future seeing available grants and funding flowing into your business account.

Show up 'as if' you have wealth

Applying the 'act as if' principle is another excellent way of boosting your confidence around money and wealth. It will help you get out of scarcity thinking and into an abundance mindset. It will get money flowing to you.

Thinking in abundance mode – 'acting as if you had money' – will help you convey the right impression as you build your business. Don't let yourself down by penny pinching to save money on items that are critical to your business success.

We are not saying you need the most expensive laptop or mobile phone, but don't come across as a cheapskate using second rate technology. Abundance thinking is called for.

Acting as if you already had money

So let's say you have to get to a business pitch a few hundred miles away. Why not invest in staying at a decent hotel the night before rather than saving a few pounds by catching the 5am milk train but arriving tired and dishevelled.

Expect wealth but don't be 'self-entitled'

On the theme of projecting success, there is a fine line between sending out the vibe that you are worthy of wealth and should be rewarded accordingly, and conveying an irritating sense of undeserved self-entitlement.

In business, if you play too small there is a danger that customers and/or stakeholders will smell desperation and anxiety. This will lead to you not attracting the rewards you deserve.

But on the other hand, stakeholders/customers will become irritated with pushy individuals whose (over) confidence is not underpinned by some talent and honest endeavour. So reflect on how you hit the sweet spot.

Make abundance thinking work for you

Intriguingly for various reasons, especially in the UK, there is often a feeling that it is not appropriate or right to strive for wealth.

There can be overt antagonism towards unattractive characters who openly flaunt their wealth in an extravagant way. We get this.

But this should not inhibit you and make you reluctant to generate wealth and build financial freedom for yourself, those around you and, should you choose to, various good causes.

Be able to convey a sense that you're comfortable around wealth and money. By developing the abundance mindset your entrepreneurial journey will be smoother.

When wealth is handled in a sensitive way this has the effect of making people feel confident around you. They will want to do business with you and build relationships rather than feeling anxious around you.

Key actions

- Cultivate an abundance, not scarcity, mindset around wealth and money.

- Identify any blockages to abundance that stand in the way of you building a healthy relationship with money.

- Think abundance not scarcity when it comes to wealth and money.

> *Cultivate an abundance, not scarcity, mindset around wealth and money.*

6: OVERCOME ADVERSITY
Highlights

Build your mental strength

Successful entrepreneurs are mentally strong. They are prepared for things not to go to plan. They are resilient and **adapt and pivot** to achieve their goals.

They are centred and comfortable in their own skin, operating with an **inner guidance system** that helps them minimise any mental friction that will slow their progress.

They have a positive outlook and **enjoy solving problems** - this comes with the territory of being an entrepreneur.

Think growth mindset

A growth mindset believes that intelligence and capabilities can be enhanced - it effortlessly **embraces change**, disruption and innovation.

The growth mindset is about **continuing development**.

In contrast the **fixed mindset is static** - it believes intelligence and capability does not have the ability to grow, evolve and respond to change.

Manage your thoughts

Master the art of resilience - managing your thoughts - when encountering setbacks. Know you will always be able to **survive**.

Acquire the art of turning negative thoughts and feelings into positive **constructive action**.

Identify with the 'motto' of the US Marines in building a strong and **resilient** mindset.

US MARINES: Improvise – Adapt – Overcome

Overcome adversity

Failures, repeated failures, are finger posts on the road to achievement. One fails forward towards success.

C S Lewis

We live in a volatile, uncertain complex and ambiguous (VUCA) world. Today security is an illusion, uncertainty is a reality and disruption is inevitable. So building the mental discipline to help cope with change and possible setbacks is a vital part of the Entrepreneur Mindset.

Wake up each day knowing that it is extremely unlikely that everything will go exactly according to plan. Be prepared for when things may go awry.

You need to be able to fall back on techniques that you have rehearsed to help you effortlessly deal with these challenges.

Learn how to develop a resilience to barriers that could block you from achieving success. Do not see yourself as a victim but someone who can learn from setbacks and succeed. It's about showing tenacity and not giving up.

Be comfortable with uncertainty

Develop mental resilience

Cultivate a growth not fixed mindset

Manage negative thoughts

Mastering the art of managing your thoughts when encountering setbacks or hurdles is critical to entrepreneurial success. You need to cultivate techniques that will help you manage any unhelpful thoughts that come across your mind when first confronted with a challenge.

Thus in dealing with adversity – building mental strength – acquire the art of turning any negative thoughts and feelings into positive constructive remedial action.

For instance let's say you were getting anxious and defeatist about the likely success of an upcoming product launch. Well here, stop the fretting. Do not let general free-floating negativity win the day.

Instead throw some energy into specific promotional activities. This will push up the probability of the event being successful.

Remember a thought is just that – it is not a reality: it can be constructively 'processed'.

Cultivate mental self-control

Resilience in the face of challenges and adversity ultimately stems from cultivating high levels of self-awareness and personal control.

Be centred

A key trait of mentally strong people is that they are 'centred' and comfortable in their own skin. They operate with a kind of Inner Guidance System that steers their attitude and behaviour.

They are determined not to let others, who do not share their vision, undercut their ambitions for the future.

They feel comfortable working on their own and are not overly concerned about having to please others.

The Choice Moment technique

Building a 'system' – process – for managing your response to people and situations is critical. Sometimes an immediate, natural, spontaneous response to a situation is the best thing to do. But in many situations it isn't.

Here, the Choice Moment technique may help. This is about reminding yourself that there is always a space – a moment – between a particular stimulus that may be calling for you to make an emotional response, and your reaction to this.

It is in this 'space' between stimulus and reaction that you need to arrive at an informed, not just a knee-jerk, response. Seize this moment to make the right choice from the range of options open to you.

Learning to intelligently exercise your Choice Moment at a point when you're receiving what you believe to be unfair negative criticism is critically important. It will buy yourself time and allow you to reflect on your optimum response.

In contrast, without the Choice Moment, you could be catapulted into a hasty, ill-thought-through immediate knee-jerk reaction. This could trigger an irretrievable long-term chain of negative events.

Responding to social media

The Choice Moment technique will help you master the challenges of having a presence on social media. It will guide how you will respond if you attract negative comments on social media from people who do not share your vision.

Hasty, emotional responses could have serious energy sapping negative long-term consequences, so stay in control and learn how to use your Choice Moment wisely before responding!

Develop a growth not fixed mindset

Developing a growth, not fixed, mindset is a must for entrepreneurs.

Those with a growth mindset:

- Have a desire to learn and will persist in the face of setbacks.
- Are receptive to innovation, change and new ideas.
- See effort as a path to mastery.
- Learn from criticism.
- Find lessons and inspiration in the success of others.
- Always learn from past failures and experiences.
- Adapt for continued success.

In contrast, those with a fixed mindset:

- ○ Believe that everything is a given and therefore become trapped in the past.

- ○ Tend to avoid challenges, get defensive and give up easily.

- ○ Often see effort as fruitless or not worthwhile.

- ○ Tend to ignore constructive feedback.

- ○ Feel threatened by the success of others.

- ○ Are resistant to new ideas.

- ○ Put up barriers to developmental transformation.

Key growth mindset questions

To help you cultivate the growth mindset, ask yourself the following questions:

> Are you constantly curious about what could be changed or improved and taking personal responsibility for solving any challenge (rather than just ignoring it)?

> If there is an improvement or change that requires extra knowledge or skill, do you have the appetite to acquire these new skills?

> Do you welcome suggestions for improvement as opposed to being non-receptive to feedback?

Enjoy effortless success – get in the flow

Successful entrepreneurs know the importance of being in the flow and not constantly fighting the tide. They know that, if they have to push too hard to make something happen, this is not sustainable over time.

We would like there to be truth in the idea that the harder you work, the more you are guaranteed to achieve your goals. But, unfortunately, life doesn't always work like that.

Intriguingly, it seems that the more attached you are to an outcome, the less likely it is to happen. Somehow anxiety grips the whole project, and this gets in the way of success.

We will be returning to this later when we talk about the importance of effortlessly operating from a position of strategic advantage, rather than endeavouring to make a flawed strategy work through endless amounts of tactical hard work and effort.

Minimise mental friction

Another dimension of getting into the flow is to minimise mental friction: remove those little irritating things that are holding you back from feeling good about an initiative.

We touched on this earlier when we spoke about persevering with an old piece of technology that is frustrating your progress, rather than treating yourself to the latest kit.

So get in the flow by doing things that create a good energy vibe that will put a spring in your step. Treat yourself to little investments that will motivate and sustain you – things that will inspire you and uplift you.

By getting rid of technology that has been a constant source of irritation and frustration you will begin to feel better about yourself. This will energise you and create that feel-good factor.

See the creative opportunity in challenges

High performers accept that uncertainty is the ongoing reality. They see an environment of constant change as one that creates opportunities. They see this as bringing out the best in them – not something to fear.

It is about embracing challenges and change and not wasting energy on complaining about things you cannot control.

Resilient individuals are prepared for things not to go according to plan. They are comfortable with the idea of adapting and pivoting in order to achieve their goals. They relate to the motto of the US Marines – Improvise, Adapt and Overcome.

Learn from setbacks

One dimension to seizing opportunities is to always learn from and not be deterred by any setbacks.

Thomas Edison, father of the light bulb, famously said, *'I've not failed 10,000 times, I've just successfully found 10,000 ways that will not work'*. This reflected his career of major triumphs but also failures.

These included the talking doll with an internal phonograph that ended up scaring children, and an electric pen which punched out what people were writing onto a template to allow for copying – but was so cumbersome it didn't catch on!

Another example is Richard Branson – he has a star-studded CV but it also includes the ill-fated Virgin Cola and Virgin Cars amongst others.

And when it comes to Elon Musk, he had several brushes with bankruptcy and faced the ignominy of being deposed as the CEO of businesses he had founded. And apparently one of his later big successes, PayPal, was voted one of the worst business ideas of 1999, but he soldiered on.

It was Nelson Mandela who said, *'The greatest glory in living lies not in never falling but in rising every time we fall.'*

Build success triggers to sustain mental strength

It's helpful to build into your day mental triggers you can use to constantly remind yourself to stay focused on the key outcomes required for entrepreneurial success.

Thus, if confidence begins to wane and self-doubt or limiting beliefs begin to kick in, you can fall back on these 'success triggers' to remind yourself to switch out of negative thinking into a more positive outcome mode.

Here we are defining success triggers as, *'Techniques that top performers use to shift their negative thinking into building natural confidence and evoking peak performance.'*

A trigger example

If you know that your energy levels dip mid-afternoon, you could set a reminder on your phone to change your environment or take a break. Then return afresh to a task with renewed energy.

Your thought management checklist

Below there are three questions to help you cultivate the resilience and tenacity required for your entrepreneurial journey.

- Do you have a mental process – a routine – to follow in converting any negative feelings that emerge into positive constructive thoughts? (This, for some, will be built into a daily mindfulness or meditation session.)

- Do you have a controlled go-to behaviour you can fall back on when confronted by a surprise or change that will avoid an overly emotional knee-jerk reaction? (Think 'Choice Moment'.)

- Do you have in place a system for measuring the extent to which you consistently operate in a growth not fixed mindset mode? (Why not revisit each of the dimensions of the growth mindset outlined above and honestly score yourself on how well you are performing on each?)

Learning lessons from adversity

We know that lots of entrepreneurs experience failures that they learn from and come out at the end the better for it.

But this begs the question: are there any fundamental lessons we can draw from how entrepreneurs learn from failure and power through the adversity they faced?

Was there a specific single signature move they followed? Is there a playbook we can follow – a menu of specific dos and don'ts to acquire a resilient mindset?

Alas, the answer is no. If it was, it would be worth its weight in gold.

All we can do here is drive home the importance of logging into the muscle memory the following fundamental *principles* for overcoming adversity.

One core principle is to cultivate that strong, centred sense that you will be able to overcome adversity. This is about believing that, although you might not have the skills in the moment to deal with an issue, you will, in time, acquire the capability to figure it out.

Another principle is being able to view setbacks as opportunities for learning and growth. You need to be able to constructively reflect on setbacks and pick out the positive lessons to be learnt and identify fresh opportunities going forward.

Finally, treat any setbacks as an opportunity to learn more about yourself. So, in your analysis of any 'failures', be honest about which were down to your own performance and which were genuinely beyond your control. In this way you will be securing learnings – experience – that will ensure you minimise the likelihood of this happening again.

Key actions

✓ Develop techniques that will help cultivate a resilient mindset, so you are able to successfully handle uncertainty and adversity.

✓ Cultivate a growth (not fixed) mindset

✓ Put in place success triggers that will constantly remind you to switch out of negativity into positive thinking mode.

→ *Successful entrepreneurs are mentally strong. They are prepared for things not to go to plan. They are resilient. They adapt and pivot to achieve their goals.*

PART TWO: CULTIVATE MENTAL RESILIENCE

Recap

Build positive beliefs

We started by dialling up the benefits of building positive beliefs. Brendon Burchard, one of the world's top coaches, does not attribute his success to any superpowers that others don't have. He sees his success as being based on his <u>belief</u> that, when a challenge arises, he will with time be able to figure it out. He'll acquire the skills and knowledge to solve this issue.

Think abundance

Here we focused on feeling comfortable around money and wealth. We positioned the process of attracting wealth as less around the acquisition of money per se and more about seeing money as an indicator of progress and success. Franklin D. Roosevelt said, *'Happiness lies not in the mere possession of money; it lies in the joy of achievement, in the thrill of creative effort.'*

Overcome adversity

We established that being able to cope with setbacks – showing tenacity and resilience – comes with the entrepreneurial territory.

At the heart of resilience is being able to solve problems. In the film *The Martian*, which is about getting Matt Damon, the hero, safely back home from Mars, one stand-out line is:

'You solve one problem. You solve the next one. And then the next. And if you solve enough problems, you get to come home. All right. Any questions?'

And still on the theme of overcoming adversity as being about solving problems – a further space illustration. This was bringing home the damaged Apollo 13 spacecraft. This is a classic example of having to 'work the problem': find a solution within a deadline, using only the resources available to you at the time. In this way. Jim Lovell (aka Tom Hanks) and his crew were safely returned to Earth.

PART THREE: TAKE DECISIVE ACTION

Overview

Action is the foundational key to all success.

Pablo Picasso

7. Boost your energy

We look at generating the energy needed to make your ideas happen. We use the word 'generated' advisedly. Energy is not a given. You need to work at being energised. So we provide you with concrete tips on how to operate in the high energy register. We focus on helping you be mentally and physically prepared so you can bring clear deep thinking and informed action to your entrepreneurial venture.

8. Commit to action

We follow this with what to many will seem an obvious point: the need to commit to massive action if you are going to make your ideas happen. But amazingly many great ideas never see the light of day because people do not act – they find all sorts of ways of procrastinating. So we provide you with techniques to make sure you become and stay action orientated.

9. Be super productive

We then look at the issue of not only being energetic and taking action but also making sure that you do this in the most productive and efficient way. As an entrepreneur, maximising the use of your time is your number one priority. So we provide you with a series of high performance tips and tricks for getting what matters most to your success achieved in the time you have available.

7: BOOST YOUR ENERGY
Highlights

Know how to generate energy

Successful entrepreneurs learn how to **create** the energy needed to achieve their goals. Energy is not just naturally given. It has to be generated.

This requires you to be on top of your **physical game** - your diet, exercise, rest & recreation and wellbeing.

But it is also about mentally thinking yourself into a high, not low, energy **state of mind.**

Get into the high energy register

There is a science emerging about how energy levels operate at different **vibrational levels.**

Have a system in place to create and **manage your energy.** Learn how to keep energy levels up even when initiatives go astray.

So think yourself into the high energy mental register. It's about being **Rocket Man/Woman.**

Manage your energy flow

Think about how **you distribute your energy** over the day.

Some entrepreneurs favour creative work in the **morning.**

Then as energy levels wane they move to management tasks in the **afternoon.**

Then **later in the day**, they focus on less demanding administrative tasks.

ENERGY MATTERS: People like to be around those who give off positive energy

Boost your energy

The world belongs to the energetic.

Ralph Waldo Emerson

Forensic energy is the platform for accurate thinking and taking action to achieve your goals.

Generate the energy needed to succeed. Know how to boost your energy and put techniques in place to help you take your energy to the next level.

In this way you will always be at the top of your physical and mental game when it comes to each entrepreneurial day.

Bring a high energy game to everything you do

Operate in the high energy register

Be a problem simplifier and energy radiator

Build a health and wellbeing platform for generating energy

If you could measure energy in terms of height, some people would be twenty feet tall and some only two feet tall.

But don't worry. If you feel your energy needs boosting the good news is that energy is not just naturally given – it can be generated.

Here the foundation for a high energy mindset is to start by being at the top of your 'physical' game – it's all about diet, exercise, sleep, rest and recreation, and wellbeing. You need a programme in place.

Approaches vary, but it's generally agreed that to be able to work consistently at a high energy level the following will pay dividends:

- Get around eight hours sleep each night.
- Follow a sensible eating plan.

- ○ Take regular exercise.

- ○ Keep hydrated.

- ○ Take breaks (every 45 minutes) through the day.

- ○ Change your working environment through the day.

- ○ Build meditation and reflection points into your day.

These are all commonsense suggestions, but often for many people not common practice. These disciplines are abandoned because of day-to-day work pressures.

Here, the key is to set up 'triggers' to remind you to follow your best practice daily routine. Some, for instance, trigger their mid-afternoon meditation ritual by setting a reminder on their phone or fitness watch. In this way, they build behaviours that become success habits.

But generating energy goes beyond being fit and healthy – you also need to 'think' yourself into the high energy register.

Get your mind into the high energy register

It is possible to think yourself into a high, not low, energy state of mind. With this mindset, you are always 'on it': present, engaged and primed to take responsibility.

Operating in this high energy register will focus you on the positive and help you manage negative forces. Being in this alert and responsive register will help you make intelligent, positive, constructive and well - thought-out responses.

In contrast, those in a low energy state of mind will be vague, indecisive, let things drift and make poorly-thought-through decisions.

Getting into the high energy register is about bringing high energy clear deep thinking to the solution of every problem that crosses your path. It's about anticipation and, if you sense anything drifting off course, taking swift corrective action. Be vigilant and on the lookout for when low energy is undercutting your performance.

Eliminate any low energy behaviours

In getting into the high energy register learn to spot and address any scenarios where you are not applying high level forensic energy to your business and its challenges.

It's about looking for those tell-tale signs that you are <u>not</u> operating with the level of energy required for entrepreneurial success, and then taking corrective action.

So be aware of the following watch outs. If you sense these coming down the track, pull that lever to get you back into high energy mode – back to being there in the moment and sorting it out!

Look out for and counter any low energy behaviours

Low energy will often manifest itself as:

A lack of precision: Tiny errors and mistakes creep into outputs and lower the confidence of stakeholders.

Lazy, sloppy, confused thinking and poor problem solving: There is a failure to distinguish between important complexity that urgently needs addressing and irrelevancies that should not be taking up your time.

A 'It's not my problem - nothing to do with me' approach to resolving issues: There is no sense of personal responsibility - you are not applying the 'buck stops here' mindset. Instead you assume that someone else will sort out issues.

No recognition of the consequences of failing to deal with a situation: Everything is done on a 'let's hope it all works out basis', rather than having a tight organised process for delivering a successful outcome.

Dilettante behaviour - dabbling in but not solving problems: There is no evidence of being a starter/finisher - someone who tenaciously commits themselves to finding a solution.

Offering token not genuine added-value creative support: When asked to help solve a problem, there is no attempt to provide a fresh perspective or substantively add value.

Manage your energy throughout the day

It's not just about having moments of excellence but <u>consistently</u> demonstrating excellence across entire projects, processes and initiatives. So, you need to have a 'system' in place that allows you to maximise your energy.

Each individual will be different. So it's not appropriate here to prescribe a one size fits all system. But you do need to reflect on when you are strongest energy-wise through the day and follow a process in order to be a high-energy performer.

For example, a system that some high-performance professionals favour is undertaking *creative* work in the morning. Then as energy levels fluctuate, in the afternoon they will then move to *management roles.* Then later in the day and in the evening they will focus on less demanding *administrative tasks.*

Protect yourself with the Bell-jar Technique

In managing your energy levels, why not try the Bell-jar Technique to help you stay in a positive, high energy register when things get tough?

In your role as an entrepreneur who is taking ownership for making things happen it is inevitable that you will attract criticism from those who do not share your vision. So, it is important that you have techniques to help you manage any negativity heading in your direction.

The Bell-jar Technique is about being able to mentally envisage pulling down a *bell-jar* over yourself when you sense that there are energy vampires around you who are undercutting your ideas and sapping your energy. This will help you stay within your own protected high energy zone.

Be a high energy leader... not a low energy follower

Cultivate the leader, not follower, mindset. It's about taking responsibility for stepping up to the plate and making things happen. Don't assume that issues will be resolved by someone else or convince yourself you don't need to take action.

This will require you to take risks, show courage and accept the consequences of putting your head above the parapet.

Know when it's down to you: the Lenny Skutnik story

In moments when I have to decide whether or not it is down to me to act in a situation to save the day I remind myself of Lenny Skutnik.

Long story short; a plane crashed into the icy Potomac River in Washington DC. Very quickly all the official rescue services were on the scene with their systems and processes for rescuing people.

But meanwhile a stewardess from the plane was in the water and close to drowning. At this point, Lenny, an office worker from nearby, decides he must act. So he dived into the river and helped the young woman to safety.

Subsequently, Lenny won various awards for bravery. But the bravery here is not just the 'physical' act of risking his life by diving into the river, it was predominately for his 'mental strength and awareness'. It was apparent to him that no one else was going to save the stewardess, so he took action.

Lenny was not an official rescue professional but he decided to take ownership – personal responsibility – for saving this woman.

Be a problem simplifier who radiates energy

It's helpful to reflect where you sit on two critical personality and capability dimensions.

The first dimension is whether you are a 'problem simplifier' who elegantly simplifies everything – as opposed to being a 'problem confuser' where everything is a muddle.

The second dimension is whether you are an 'energy radiator', who does everything with enthusiasm in a way that uplifts those around them – as opposed to being an 'energy drain' who saps everyone's enthusiasm.

Put these two ideas together, and you can see that, as a successful entrepreneur, you need to be a 'problem simplifier' who is also an 'energy radiator' with whom people enjoy working.

You don't want to be an 'energy drain' who is also a 'problem confuser' – someone who puts noise, confusion and hesitancy into every process whilst at the same time draining the energy of everyone around them.

So strive to be a high energy 'problem simplifier' who always shows up with their A-Game and a can-do attitude.

A High Performance Framework

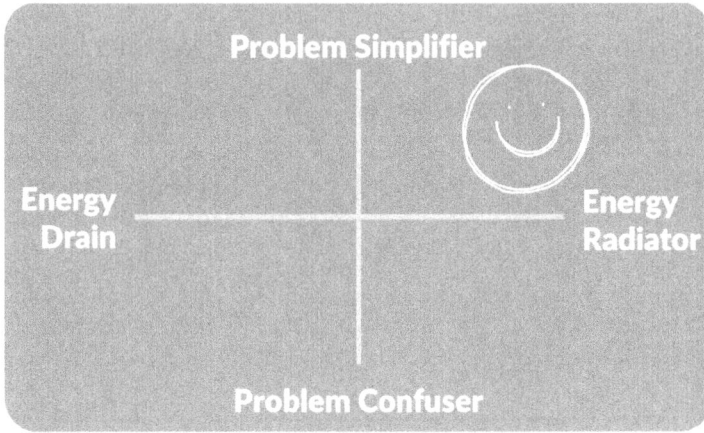

The pay-off from boosting your energy

Keeping up your physical and mental energy levels is vital in your entrepreneurial journey. There is nothing more frustrating than small lapses in concentration and momentary intellectual laziness – cognitive miserliness in thinking things through – leading to a disaster that comes back to haunt you.

You need the energy to always turn up with your A-Game – the best version of yourself. And if things go wrong, you will need to find that little extra in the reserve tank and be the person who steps up to the plate and sorts things out.

So don't be the person with low energy levels who just lets things drift and assumes that someone else will step in to put things right.

Commit to being the person who can always apply high levels of forensic energy in any situation. This will deliver massive benefits.

Key actions

✓ Build a strong wellbeing platform to help you generate energy.

✓ Get into the high energy register and apply maximum forensic energy to every situation.

✓ Strive to be an energy radiator and problem simplifier.

→ *Get yourself into the high energy mental register. Energy is not a given – it needs to be generated.*

8: COMMIT TO ACTION
Highlights

Start now – be bold

Taking massive, determined action is crucial to entrepreneurial success - be **action orientated**.

Turn ideas into action. Don't procrastinate around great entrepreneurial ideas.

It's all down to you to **make things happen**.

Act decisively and often

Don't just be busy - focus on taking action to **deliver outcomes** to progress your business goals.

Think of yourself as the General with the **Executive Vision**. Acquire the big picture overview of the actions needed to secure victory.

Make sure you **commit to taking action**. You should always have lots of upcoming actions in your calendar or journal. Monitor your progress in achieving key actions.

Learn as you go

Successful entrepreneurs learn as they progress. They embrace the **build the plane** as you fly it - adapt as you go - principle.

Entrepreneurs make taking action a **habit**.

They set up triggers to **build and reinforce** success habits.

STEVE MARABOLI: 'Excuses are a time thief. Have a goal, accept responsibility, and take action'

Commit to action

The path to success is to take massive, determined action.

Tony Robbins

The world's top business coaches tell us that taking action on what matters most is the single most important determinant of entrepreneurial success.

Be the kind of person who having had an idea will always start doing something about it: putting strategies, plans and tactics in place to get their idea off the ground.

You need to be someone who makes things happen. Move away from being someone who has an idea but never quite gets to the point of taking action to deliver this.

Start – focus on the how later

Learn from your actions and adjust as you go

Be consistently excellent in everything you do

Take personal responsibility – ownership – for action

Always step up to the plate and be the person who will take control and act to deal with events. Develop the leader/commander mentality: take personal responsibility for resolving issues.

We live in an era where, in the face of adversity, there is often a tendency to blame others and/or expect others to have taken action, rather than to take personal responsibility for sorting out the situation yourself.

Take action in the face of uncertainty

Entrepreneurs make a start even though the precise way forward with a particular venture may not be totally clear.

They accept that the future is always full of surprises. So, rather than waiting for a detailed plan of exactly how to reach a specific goal to materialise, they set off with just a general sense of their direction and adjust enroute.

This is in contrast to those who delay taking action: they spend an inordinate amount of time pondering on exactly how to take that *perfect* first step.

They are endlessly waiting for a step-by-step playbook – roadmap – of precisely what to do next to manifest itself. This, of course, never arrives!

Make a start – worry about the 'how' later

Yes: entrepreneurs are good at getting started – always taking that first step, then adjusting enroute. Some call this the *'build the plane as you fly it'* principle. It is all about starting and adapting as you go. For example, this is how Airbnb evolved.

Entrepreneurs do not obsess on the 'how'. They don't worry about having the exact plans in place of how to get there – these will evolve.

It's about getting underway even though you do not have a fully developed plan in place. This entrepreneurial approach is a counterpoint to more traditional cautious approaches to business. The successful entrepreneur's motto is, 'D*on't let the process kill the big idea.'*

The train and boat analogy

One way of thinking about the entrepreneurial way of taking action in the face of uncertainty is to draw the distinction between a train journey and a voyage by boat.

For a train journey, you arrive at a station, follow a set pattern of travel from station to station along a predetermined rail route.

Compare this with making a voyage by sailing boat. Here you have a general sense of the direction in which you are heading but need to constantly adjust for wind, tide and 'events' as you travel.

Illustration: Dog Treats

An entrepreneur's approach to taking action

Let's take the example of someone who wants to set up an online business selling accessories for dogs – coats, leads, beds etc. The traditional approach would be to do research to test all the different products and service opportunities. Then spend time designing an 'all singing and dancing' website.

The more entrepreneurial – act in the face of uncertainty – approach would be to *get started*: set up a basic website, start to sell some products and then adapt your product range and customer service strategy based on customer feedback. It is about starting with a minimal offering and building the business out from there.

Apply simultaneous not sequential thinking

Entrepreneurs push ahead on many fronts. They take constant, *simultaneous*, decisive action to achieve different end goals.

This is different from people who operate *sequentially* where no action at all is taken to start task B until task A has been fully completed.

But this advice comes with a health warning. Don't confuse the idea of simultaneously tackling your agenda for the day with the idea of frenetically hopping between tasks with no one task ever being given your full 100% concentration.

Act with excellence

The propensity to take action is critical but this needs to be accompanied with a commitment to excellence in the execution of each action.

Studies show that this commitment to excellence is important because it taps into a primal source of intrinsic human motivation.

So when it comes to excellence, you need to not only live up to your customers' expectations – but also meet your <u>own</u> high standards.

Being good at what you do helps shape a sense of who you are, and frames your identity.

Vince Lombardi said, *'The quality of a person's life is in direct proportion to their commitment to excellence, regardless of their chosen field of endeavour.'*

Therefore, it is not surprising that successful entrepreneurs take personal responsibility for constantly improving their capability. They develop an obsession with the ongoing mastery of the key skills that will power them towards achieving their goals.

In sum, it's not just about taking action, it's also about always doing this to the very best of your ability. Jessica Guidobono said, *'Every job is a self-portrait of the person who did it. Autograph your work with excellence.'*

Know who needs your A-Game – honour the struggle

Know when to turn up with your A-Game and be the go-to linchpin who will act to resolve issues. You need to be able to do this even when you're not feeling particularly buoyant or on top of your game.

Recognise that there will be moments when it is simply a matter of digging in and doing the hard yards to keep the show on the road.

Elton John doesn't just rock up to a gig and play his standard set. He may be feeling below par and/or have lots of day-to-day things going on in his life. But he believes that he has a duty (responsibility) to put these out of his mind and provide each particular audience during his tour with the most memorable experience possible.

Make taking action a habit – set up success triggers

We have referred to setting up success triggers and it is good practice to start thinking about how to use triggers to build the habit of always taking action, rather than letting matters drift.

One example of a trigger to prompt action would be to ensure you can always see your potential actions scheduled in your calendar. This creates a daily focus on - and commitment to – taking action.

Get actions you are 'thinking' about taking out of your head and into your diary so you can see these actions in a timeline.

Another example of a success trigger to nudge you into the action habit is, before stopping work for the day, to always write the <u>first sentence of the next section</u> of say a business communication that you plan to continue the following day. This will spur you into action in the morning and engrain the action habit.

The action habit drives success

Without question acquiring the action habit is at the heart of the Entrepreneur Mindset. Successful entrepreneurs always show up and take action.

So if something needs doing, and even if they don't feel like doing it, they still step up to the plate and take action. They know if things go wrong that ultimately it's always their fault!

It is easy when you have so many activities on your to-do list to avoid action and default to a 'hope for the best' strategy. This is a mistake. Recognise that it is always your responsibility to act and sort things out.

Moreover it is not just about acting but always doing so with excellence. Do not just go through the motions. Autograph your work with excellence.

Be the best possible version of what you are capable of achieving – someone who acts with consistent excellence.

Key actions

Be action orientated – totally committed to action. Do not delay or procrastinate around great entrepreneurial ideas.

Get started without worrying about how to get there, then course correct as you go.

Take personal responsibility for owning problems and always showing up with excellence – your A-Game.

Turn great entrepreneurial ideas into action. Don't procrastinate!

9: BE SUPER PRODUCTIVE
Highlights

Make the time

Successful entrepreneurs are super productive – **high performers** – in getting things done quickly.

As an entrepreneur you can't fall back on the excuse that there was not enough time. It's about always 'creating' the time. Having focus and prioritising will give you **eight days a week**.

Consistently deliver **excellence**, even when you are up against the clock.

Get organised and prioritise

High productivity is about developing an **organised mind** – not just muddling through.

But it's primarily about focus – working on **the things that matter most** ahead of the things that aren't as important.

Apply the principle of **block time**. Start each day by allocating 90 minutes to the most important task. Focus on this big-ticket issue.

Be a starter – and a finisher

Tackle procrastination – get started. **Eat that frog before breakfast!** Take a small step, enjoy your progress – this will sustain your willpower.

Don't self-sabotage – **cut distractions** that disrupt your progress. Free yourself from any demons like constantly checking your inbox.

Look out for perfectionism. Know when it is time to let it go. Don't over-engineer everything. **Laugh in the face of perfection.**

TAME DISTRACTIONS: Develop your focus, be clear on your purpose and act decisively

Be super productive

Productivity isn't about being a workhorse, keeping busy or burning the midnight oil, it's more about priorities, planning and fiercely protecting your time.

Margarita Tartakovsky

Successful entrepreneurs are super productive – high performers – when it comes to taking action. They don't fall back on the excuse that there was not enough time. They find ways of getting critical things done.

Being productive isn't about using techniques and apps for being organised and managing your time. These help but it is primarily about cultivating the high productivity mindset – and making this a habit.

Time management and organisational techniques have a role to play. But the bigger issue is getting your mindset right. Ensure that you start each day with a clear purpose and always act with intentionality. Don't just shuffle into the day and sleepwalk through events in a haphazard way.

And at the core of the high productivity mindset is always *focusing,* prioritising and making sure you are always working on what matters most.

High productivity is about mindset

The key to productivity is to focus in block time

Be a starter and finisher

Focus on what matters most

High productivity begins with having total clarity on the things you need to accomplish in order to deliver a priority outcome.

Highly productive entrepreneurs ruthlessly focus on the important issues. They cut out all unimportant activities. They work on the things that matter most and will make a difference. They develop a laser-like focus on what they should be doing to bring in that next customer and improve profit and drive growth. They do not get deflected into time-wasting, energy-sapping activities.

Thus, a *focused* business owner has a clear purpose, and always acts with intention – focusing on the priority goals. They are constantly asking whether what they are doing is helping them to achieve their business goals?

Compare this with an *unfocused* business owner who is always firefighting and just reacting to events, and not focusing on the key drivers of success. He/she has no clear strategic focus and does not think through whether or not the activities they are being plunged into will achieve a key end outcome.

When it comes to focusing on what matters most a good practice tip is to ask yourself, *'Is what I am about to do over the <u>next hour</u> going to help me achieve one of my goals?'*

Sometimes you have to say No

One of the big challenges for the small business owner is an anxiety to please. You feel you have to say yes to everything – even if it is not profitable – because you fear you might not get more work.

Another issue is being tempted into taking on too many commitments that are not directly related to building your business, such as running local business get-togethers. This could be a great networking opportunity but it could become a time sink. So think carefully before automatically saying yes.

Be prepared to cut things out

Cut out activities that you may have started but that on review do not seem to be going anywhere – and are beginning to sap your energy. Rethink how – and when – you will re-engage with these.

Do not simply aimlessly drift on with activities in the vague hope that something will turn up. We know that insanity, according to Einstein, lies in *'doing the same thing over and over and expecting different results.'*

Focus on the core success drivers

Successful strategic entrepreneurs focus their time on the core drivers of success, and are not deflected into less important, nice to do, marginal issues. They focus on those factors that will 'move the needle' and make their business a success.

This could be improving the quality of your product or it could be about improving your customer experience. But it is unlikely to be rearranging the filing system.

Prioritise the motivator factors

Concentrate on the *motivator* factors – what it is that truly drives customer choice and satisfaction – ahead of the *hygiene* factors that everyone expects to get from a product or service as a matter of course.

Zero in on profit generating activities

Focus on activities that will generate profit and ensure you have sufficient cash flow. Don't be tempted to take on vanity projects that don't make money. And, if the short term priority is winning more customers, don't get involved in costly fancy long-term brand-building exercises.

What to do each morning: Start with the big rocks

Start each day by focusing on the *big rocks*. The big rocks are the things that, if you don't do them immediately, will lead to bad consequences.

Then, when these are sorted, focus on the *medium rocks* – delivering these will excite and delight the customer and make them an advocate for your business.

And then, only when you have worked through the big and the medium rocks, do you focus on all the *little rocks* – things that need doing but are not central to driving your business forward.

The point of this analogy is that many small business owners wake up each morning and start on the little rock issues – the small things - in the hope that later in the day they will get to the medium and big rocks. But this rarely happens. By the end of the day, they have only completed the unimportant tasks.

Know how to delegate

On the theme of focusing on success drivers, get your delegation strategy right. Some business owners do too much themselves – they under-delegate.

Others over-delegate: they expect people to do tasks that are beyond them – things that the business owner should really undertake themselves.

Take control of your time and space

Highly productive people are ruthless and decisive in managing their time and environment.

Watch out for time thieves and energy drains

Successful entrepreneurs don't let time and energy robbers deflect them away from what they want to achieve.

They are ruthless in protecting their time and energy. They are not afraid to create barriers to entry. So, limit how accessible you are so you can focus.

Don't let your inbox drive your agenda and control your diary

Take control of your own day. Don't let crazy-makers, energy vampires and timewasters rent space in your head!

Don't immediately look at your inbox each morning. Get done what you want to achieve before you respond to others.

In today's social media and email environment it is easy to start the day by tackling 58 outstanding emails or checking Facebook, Twitter, WhatsApp or LinkedIn messages. But this is a mistake – it is important to start the day by tackling your own agenda.

Begin each day by dealing with the key 'big rock' issues that need attending to: do not be distracted by the inbox.

In sum, organise your diary and your day in a way that suits you and is not determined by others.

Apply the principle of 'block time' to undertake deep work

One specific tip when it comes to organising your day is not to let constant interruptions get in the way of you getting stuff done.

An interruption may only be 15 seconds long, but this can disrupt your overall flow state and make tasks that could be completed in 30 minutes take hours.

So in tackling a key task it becomes important to carve out a block of time and to give this your undivided attention, without any interruptions.

A top tip is to start each day by allocating *90 minutes* to the most important task for the day. Don't be side-tracked until the big-ticket issue for the day has been nailed.

Get into the high productivity flow state

When it comes to getting in the zone to do 'deep work', there are three factors to consider. You need to think about with whom you are working, where you are working and the time when you will work.

People: Decide how much time you want to spend with different types of people. You want to be working with energetic people who simplify problems. You don't want to be working with energy-sapping people who confuse and complicate things.

Place: Choose the most productive places to work – ones that give you inspiration. If possible, change the location of your work periodically. Different people will favour differing locations for helping them get in the flow. Some favour working in their kitchen or home office. Others may prefer to work at Starbucks and others overlooking the ocean.

Time: Pick your most productive times. Don't let other people force you into activities that require peak performance at a time that doesn't suit you. Different people are strongest and most creative at different points in the day. Also, work on activities for no more than 30-40 minutes before you walk around or introduce a change of pace - so you return refreshed.

Overcome the procrastination trap

A major productivity challenge is procrastination – delaying getting started. Many people find it difficult to take the first step and get underway – they keep putting off what it is they know they should be doing. So it is important to foster techniques to offset a tendency to procrastinate.

Be a starter finisher

Be tenacious: follow through on your initial actions to make things happen. Recognise that things rarely happen with just one instruction, or communication. You need to have the energy to progress chase projects and people to drive successful outcomes.

One qualification is that procrastination can sometimes be our friend. It could be our intuition telling us to hold off until the time is right. But, in most situations, procrastination just blocks our progress and success.

Get it in the calendar

It is good practice, as we stressed earlier, to ensure that the activities needed to achieve an outcome are diarised – put in the calendar. The act of writing down the date and time when you will be tackling an action means that it's more likely to happen.

Eat the frog before breakfast

Don't put off doing things you don't necessarily enjoy. Front up to difficult tasks at the beginning of the day. Sometimes you have to eat that frog before breakfast!

Where there's a WAY there's a WILL

Be bold in always taking the first step. Commit to action and apply the principle of 'where there's a <u>way</u> there's a <u>will</u>!'

Make a start, get underway, then because you are seeing results from having taken this initial action, you will have the motivation – and will – to continue.

Many people wait for the motivation *before* they act. But this is the wrong way of thinking about it. If you take some action this will trigger the motivation to continue. So it's action leading to motivation. Not the other way round.

Go public and commit

Why not commit in public to achieving certain deadlines. This builds on your intrinsic motivation by committing to an extrinsic deadline – one you need to meet if you do not want to let people down.

Use placeholders to overcome mental blocks

High performers keep focused on the end outcome and find ways to avoid letting mental blocks get in the way of achieving their goal.

For example, musicians when writing a song, often use the placeholder technique. They may not know exactly what lyrics to use next as they develop the song. So, they put in a placeholder and keep going with the musical composition. Apparently, Paul McCartney's placeholder for *Yesterday* was 'scrambled eggs'!

Build in elapsed time

A number of writers believe in the power of allowing the subconscious to 'work' on an emerging idea overnight. Stephen King – when he is stuck in his writing – refers to leaving it to *'The boys in the basement'*. He sleeps on the idea and next morning his subconscious has come up with the solution.

Take breaks

Creative people build in breaks every 45 minutes or so to get re-energised. Einstein used to regularly go for walks to help him progress an idea.

Look out for the perfectionist syndrome

Clearly it is important to produce quality outcomes. You do not want to let sub-standard work out of the door. But you can reach a point where the extra percentage point of quality is not worth the time delay.

An obsession with constantly polishing an output on the grounds that it is not quite ready to be released to the public is unhealthy. To be super productive you need to know when it is time for lift off: launch.

Don't wait for the moment when everything is perfect – just let it go! One film director famously said: *'films don't ever get finished; they just get released!'*

So, don't over-engineer everything. When it is good enough, 'fling it to the public'. *Laugh in the face of perfection!*

It's about getting the speed/quality balance right. 98% right in an hour can usually be better than 100% right in four hours (not always but mostly).

Jeff Bezos tells us that in the early days of building the Amazon empire, he had to learn to be comfortable making decisions with only about 60% of the information he thought he ideally needed for sound informed decision-making.

Monitor your productivity

It is helpful to set up a journal and keep a record of your productivity. By monitoring what works and what doesn't you will gradually build up a picture of how to work smarter and faster.

Individuals will have different monitoring approaches. But you could ask yourself at the end of the week if you have reached level 9 or 10 (good), or only level 1 or 2 (poor) in completing an initiative on time to a high quality and with the minimum of friction.

Learn lessons: Know what works and doesn't work

Don't let history repeat itself by keeping going with the same inefficient behaviour but expecting to get different results. This seems a simple enough principle to follow.

However, some business owners cannot let things go because they may have sunk so much emotional energy into an idea. So they keep persevering rather than terminating the project.

If things are not working, have the confidence to do a U-turn and do something different that will work.

Develop a system for processing information

Highly productive entrepreneurs will have a clearly thought-out system for processing information and do not succumb to 'information overwhelm'.

One approach is to develop the skill of identifying the key concept – the big idea – underpinning an incoming piece of information, and documenting this. Then see if this 'insight' prompts constructive ideas that can be applied in your own business.

But it doesn't stop here. As more information arrives – concepts and big ideas – you then 'progressively summarise' these into *meta-concepts* that could provide powerful business lessons.

So, it's an organised process of constantly reducing incoming material down to its essence and applying these core principles – ideas and concepts – you have curated to your business.

Make high productivity your super power

As an entrepreneur seeking to turn ideas into action your most precious commodity is your own time. It is staggering to compare and contrast what a highly productive individual can get through in a day compared to someone who, in the same 24 hour period, will hardly achieve anything.

Thus if you are running a business having super productivity will give you a massive competitive advantage. And, if you are working within an organisation, this will help you effortlessly achieve key milestones. Similarly, if you are working on that personal project or good-cause venture, high productivity is the key to seeing everything come to fruition.

Here, the platform for being super productive is having an organised mind – coupled with the ability to focus on what matters most and then always acting with purpose and intentionality to achieve your goals.

To support these core productivity principles, you can then apply specific techniques such as working uninterrupted on priority tasks for the first 90 minutes of the day – the block time principle. This will help put you in the high productivity club.

Key actions

✓ Focus with purpose on what matters most.

✓ Recognise the preciousness of time and the importance of protecting yourself from 'crazy makers' – time thieves and energy robbers.

✓ Apply the 90 minute block time principle each morning.

→ *Focus on the things that matter most and protect your time.*

PART THREE: TAKE DECISIVE ACTION

Recap

Boost your energy

We explained that successful entrepreneurs ooze high energy. They recognise that top athletes do not just rock up at the Olympics in the hope of winning a gold medal. They follow a health, fitness and mental wellbeing regime to generate energy. Bill Gates gets into the 'high energy register' by getting seven hours sleep a night, starting his day on the treadmill, and building meditation and downtime into his day. Apparently, he enjoys unloading the dishwasher – it helps him to unwind!

Commit to action

We looked then at taking personal responsibility for taking action. Seek out exemplars of action taking in practice. Long before the film about the plane making an emergency landing in New York's Hudson River, I had become a fan of the pilot Sullenberger. Why? Because he took full responsibility for deciding what to do and then acting. And he did this in the face of the contrary advice coming in from air traffic controllers.

Be super productive

We reviewed the need to be highly productive. Here we looked at how Jeff Bezos, Bill Gates, Richard Branson, Elon Musk, Warren Buffett et al operate - there are a few standout common features.

They all report focusing on what matters most. They set aside a 'golden hour' each day for top priorities, guaranteeing themselves 250 hours per year of top quality time on key issues.

Next, when engaged in any one activity, they give this and everyone around them their 100% total focus and attention. They don't flip-flop around, half-listening and half-thinking about something else.

And finally they are ruthless in stopping doing things that are not moving them towards their goals. So you could do worse as an aspiring entrepreneur than to borrow from these top entrepreneurs' playbook.

PART FOUR: APPLY CLEAR THINKING
Overview

Man's greatness lies in his power of thought.

Blaise Pascal

10. Embrace strategic excellence

Taking effective entrepreneurial action requires prior clear, deep thinking. Clear thinking makes for bold and decisive action. Fuzzy thinking leads to hesitancy and inaction. And one area where clear thinking is called for is in ensuring you are making the right strategic decisions. This is what we focus on in this chapter.

It is very difficult to turn ideas into action if you are playing in the wrong space and constantly battling the tide. If you want to achieve success in an effortless way then start each day with the advantage of being in the right strategic place.

11. Provide simple solutions

We look at applying clear thinking to the generation of simple solutions. The aim is to avoid unnecessary complexity, complication and confusion. So think simple. This will smooth your path in turning your ideas into action.

12. Apply business acumen

You want to take your idea forward but this needs to be in a financially sustainable way. So here we look at applying business acumen. It is easy to get caught up in the excitement of having a really imaginative idea, but not putting in the clear thinking needed to ensure you are working with a sound business model.

10: EMBRACE STRATEGIC EXCELLENCE
Highlights

Strategic thinking

Be a **strategic entrepreneur** (who knows where to play, how to win and how to get there with the minimum of resources).

Do not be an **opportunity seeker** (who is rushing around chasing lots of possibilities in a tactical way).

Identify the key success drivers and tackle hidden obstacles

Pinpoint what will make the **biggest difference**: identify the most important determinants of success.

Develop a nose for teasing out any hidden obstacles that are blocking your expansion and **fix these big-ticket issues** as a priority.

It's about **working on what matters most**. Avoid getting deflected into time-wasting, energy-sapping activities.

The most efficient route

Successful entrepreneurs pinpoint the **optimum route** to success using the minimum of resources.

Don't take the scenic route - **go direct!**

Focus your resources on what is most likely to deliver results.

WOOD – NOT TREES: Avoid falling into the trap of being too busy to see what it is you should really be working on

10: Embrace strategic excellence

It's difficult to tactically retrieve a flawed strategic position.

Rich Schefren

Make sure you maximise the chances of being successful by picking a space in the market where you will excel.

Think through clearly and deeply how you will strategically position yourself – your brand – in the optimum way.

Select a market positioning that will reinforce the strengths of your business. Think strategically about your use of time. Focus your time on what will deliver critical outcomes. Put energy into the key determinants of success.

Strategic superiority beats tactical effort

Pinpoint and fix major blocks and constraints

Know which strategic levers to pull for business success

Be sure you have a compelling idea

Some entrepreneurs get so carried away with their own idea that they fail to take any soundings about how attractive their offer actually is to their potential target market.

They do not rigorously assess whether they really do have a compelling idea that is meeting some form of unmet need. Thus many start-ups make the rookie error of creating a solution to a problem that doesn't really exist.

A start point for assessing whether you have a compelling idea is to ask yourself whether your idea is providing a fundamental benefit.

Do not try to foist on the world a half-baked 'idea' that does not offer a genuine benefit.

Importantly not all ideas need to be massive breakthroughs. But as a minimum you need to ensure that the potential of your idea does not just exist in your own head.

It must go beyond just being something you have become emotionally attached to. You need an idea that genuinely provides an innovative, imaginative extra added-value product and/or service benefit. It needs to offer a dimension that will give you some form of competitive advantage.

Illustration: The Driving Glove – a solution to a non-problem

A concrete example of a poor idea – a solution that was not based on a genuine problem – was the pitch in the Dragons' Den to secure investment for a *right-handed* driving glove.

The 'idea' behind it was that UK drivers would wear this glove when travelling in Europe to remind them to keep on the right hand side of the road.

We can't repeat what the Dragons thought about this as a business idea. It did, though, do slightly better than fitting artificial soft claws in different colours to your pet cat!

So make sure you have <u>not</u> come up with a solution that is looking for a problem.

Do some basic market research

In the beginning many entrepreneurs will not have the resources to commission a full scale market research project to assess likely customer reaction to their idea. But as a minimum you should take some informal soundings with potential customers from your target market.

Combine this with your own judgement to make an informed assessment of the strength and power of your idea.

Here, the *Jobs to be Done* framework is a useful way of getting critical customer feedback.

So, for example, if you were thinking of introducing a payment system for retailers to use to collect money from customers, why not interview customers who currently use a competitor service.

Ask them the following questions to pinpoint what *job it is that has to be done for your own new product to be successful*.

So the questions could be along the lines of:

In using this product, what job do you want done?

What are you always hoping to achieve?

Why is achieving this particular job important to you?

What does success look like if this job is done?

What does it look like if the job is not done?

In seeking to get the job done, what have you looked at and tried? What did you learn from this?

Of all the different features and benefits that products offer to do the job in the way you want, which of these is the most important and why?

By asking these few simple but powerful questions, you will quickly establish whether your product idea has legs. Does it do the job?

In this case it will probably be a product that customers trust, makes transactions easy, works with existing systems, isn't too expensive, helps manage fraud and provides first-class customer service.

The *Jobs to be Done* framework will serve you well.

Make sure you are in the right strategic place

The golden rule is always 'play where you are most likely to win'. Seek out a strategic market position that will maximise your chances of success.

Be totally clear on the battleground on which you want to compete.

A lot of businesses end up *shuffling* into existence without thinking about their strategic positioning. The result is that their day-to-day existence becomes about tactically trying to retrieve a flawed strategic positioning. They end up spending each day firefighting.

For example, if you are a retail outlet in a side street with limited footfall, even though you have a superb product and excellent service, you are probably going to struggle.

In contrast, a retail outlet that is in the optimum location, even with an inferior product and service to yours, is likely to succeed. Their strategic positioning gives them an unassailable competitive advantage.

A strong strategic competitive positioning means not always having to say Yes

One advantage of a sound competitive positioning is that you will have the confidence to know when to say *Yes,* and when to say *No* to potential business opportunities.

If you have little strategic competitive advantage you end up saying Yes to non-profitable work that becomes a time sink that drains your energy.

Strategic excellence will help you <u>create</u> not just <u>chase</u> demand

In an ideal world you position your offer - the value and benefits you provide - in a way that draws people towards you. In other words you *create* a demand for your particular product or service.

This is in sharp contrast with *chasing* demand where you are constantly having to cut costs and compete on price.

So the aim should be to provide a valued set of benefits to *create* something that people will come to you to buy, rather than having to always *chase* demand in a race to the bottom on price.

Identify the levers that move the needle

We have introduced the idea of focusing on what matters most to your business and putting all of your energy into working on the critical success drivers. Ensure you are always working on issues that are most likely to 'move the success needle'.

Pinpoint any hidden constraints

Successful entrepreneurs have a nose for pinpointing any hidden obstacles that are blocking their expansion and fix this as a priority. They are always looking to identify the fastest most efficient route to success using the minimum of resources. They go direct – they don't take the scenic route!

Example of strategic thinking: We need a bigger oven!

Let's take a business selling takeaway pizzas. To improve profits the owner has sent his chef on courses to improve the speed with which he can produce the pizzas.

He has also invested in training for improving the speed of customer service. And he has looked at the supply chain to source lower cost ingredients.

You get the idea: all the 'tactical' thinking and action has been done.

But the single biggest barrier - constraint - to growth has not been addressed. This centres on the need for a bigger pizza oven!

If you can only produce four pizzas in one bake, then this is the big constraint that needs to be addressed. All the other initiatives are *nice to have* but oven size is the critical (hidden) constraint to expansion and growth.

Review opportunities for leverage

Know how to leverage: invest in and maximise the use of key resources that will give you the greatest return.

So one leverage point could be your ability to utilise automation and technology. Another illustration is focusing on any specialist/unique knowledge in a particular area that is superior to everyone else. A further leverage example could be your expertise in accessing funds to finance growth.

So the action point here is to reflect on where you can leverage your business to maximum advantage. Use this to drive your business.

Gain strategic advantage by understanding your customers

We have looked at the power of talking to your potential customers in deciding whether or not you have a viable idea. Let's continue this theme of looking at your idea through the lens of the customer with a view to teasing out insights that could give you a strategic advantage.

Apply the 80/20 rule

Successful businesses identify their most profitable customers and focus their offer on this niche rather than trying to cover the complete spectrum.

The 80/20 rule tells us that the top 20% of customers usually generate 80% of the profit of a business.

Focus on areas that are important to customers

To help you stay focused on what is important to customers it is useful to set up a satisfaction and importance matrix. This allows you to plot the key feature of your offer on two dimensions.

First, the level of customer satisfaction your product achieves on a feature and, secondly, the importance of this feature to the customer.

This kind of matrix helps you clarify your thinking on where you should be focusing your efforts. A diagrammatic illustration of what this might look like for a business is shown below:

So, in this example, this business would:

> Focus on priorities by improving performance on the high importance features that have low customer satisfaction scores.

> Maintain high performance by continuing to offer excellent customer satisfaction on these high importance features.

> Check for any overengineering on low importance features, where there is high customer satisfaction.

> Assign a low priority to features that have low customer satisfaction scores, and are of low importance to the customer.

Build strategic excellence via sound competitive positioning

Another perspective to help you ensure you are in the right strategic place is to understand – in relation to your offer – what your competitors are doing.

Identify strategic competitive threats and opportunities

One technique to help work out your best strategic position is:

- o Select your biggest *competitor*.

- o Identify the *threats* that this competitor could pose for you.

- o Then identify the *opportunities* you have to challenge or compete successfully against this competitor.

This will help you decide where to shore up your defences, and where you can *attack* your competitors.

Create a competitive positioning statement

It is helpful to prepare a *competitive positioning statement* to help select the right battleground. This describes how your offer – brand – differs from key competitors and will help you shape your Unique Selling Proposition (USP).

Specifically identify your:

Market offer: the category in which you are competing.

Target audience: who your offer is aimed at.

Brand discriminators: the factors that explain how and why customers choose between different brands.

Brand differentiators*:* where you enjoy differentiation from your competitors on the key brand discriminators.

Brand personality: what your brand is promising.

Core customer proposition: the core benefits you are offering.

This will help you draft out a statement that sums up your offer and helps you think clearly about your strategy.

Illustration: Creating a competitive positioning statement

Let's take an illustration of how a commercial photography business might use this framework.

Market offer: Commercial photography.

Target audience: Commercial businesses prepared to pay a premium price for transformational creative solutions and outstanding customer service.

Brand discriminators: Leading-edge technical skill in commercial photography and the ability to come up with innovative solutions.

Brand differentiators: Outstanding technical expertise coupled with creativity plus an extraordinarily high level of customer service.

Brand personality: High levels of creativity, originality, energy and enthusiasm coupled with accessible technical knowhow.

Core customer proposition: Our technical expertise, passion and creativity combine to deliver photography with that extra edge.

How this photography business could apply its competitive positioning statement to its next marketing decisions

This competitive positioning statement allows this photography business to make intelligent decisions about:

The assignments to say yes to:

Where there is a willingness to pay a premium price for working in partnership to create innovative commercial photography that goes beyond just being technically proficient.

The assignments to say no to:

Where the focus is primarily on producing technically sound photography on a limited budget with little commitment to creativity.

Be a strategic entrepreneur not an opportunity seeker

A helpful way to sum up what we have been saying about the importance of strategic positioning is to understand the distinction between a 'strategic entrepreneur' and someone who we might describe as an 'opportunity seeker'.

Strategic entrepreneurs position themselves in the optimum strategic place and focus on what matters most – what moves the needle.

Opportunity seekers are always rushing around chasing lots of possibilities in a tactical way.

So strive to become a strategic entrepreneur who knows *'where to play, how to win and how to get there with the minimum of resources'*.

Strategic excellence makes for effortless success

Strategic excellence starts with taking time out to *'think'*. It is difficult to bring an idea to fruition – even with lots of hard work – if you have not carefully thought through where you should position yourself in the marketplace for maximum strategic advantage.

You need to give detailed thought to exactly where to play, how you build a competitive advantage and how to deliver your idea in an economical way using the minimum of resources (following a sound business model).

Do not be an entrepreneur who is always rushing around chasing lots of different possibilities in a tactical way, hoping honest endeavour will make it work.

Instead be a strategic entrepreneur who applies clear deep thinking to ensure that what you are doing provides maximum competitive advantage.

Key actions

✓ Apply strategic thinking: play where you are most likely to win.

✓ Focus on the core drivers of success: what matters most.

✓ Identify and tackle any hidden obstacles that are restricting your growth.

> *Be a strategic entrepreneur who knows where to play, how to win and how to get there with the minimum of resources. Avoid being an opportunity seeker who chases possibilities in a purely tactical way.*

11: PROVIDE SIMPLE SOLUTIONS
Highlights

Simplicity is the ultimate sophistication

Successful entrepreneurs are alert to the **dangers of overengineering** their product or service. They cut out bells and whistles that don't add value.

Constantly think about **lean and agile** ways of getting to the end result.

Find ways of effortlessly creating and delivering your final product or service to customers. **Keep it simple.**

Think Occam's Razor

Entrepreneurs know that **'All things being equal the simplest solution is usually the best'.**

It's all about providing customer friendly, **simple to understand** - and use - solutions.

Constantly **review your processes** to remove any unnecessary complexity, confusion or fuss.

Build a minimum viable product

MVP

Start with a minimum viable version of your offer - providing only the **must-have features**.

Then build out the features required to give you a competitive advantage - to arrive at the **optimum offer.**

Arrive at a **simple, elegant and effective solution** that customers love - and one that makes the best use of your resources.

LESS IS MORE: *'I just have to chisel away the superfluous material.'*
Michelangelo on sculpting a masterpiece

Provide simple solutions

Simplicity is the ultimate sophistication.

Steve Jobs

The ability to consistently deliver simple solutions is a key part of entrepreneurial success. Do not overcomplicate your product or service. You need to create simple customer solutions: streamline your product or service.

Einstein said, *'Everything should be made as simple as possible, but not simpler.'* Eliminate unhelpful 'confusion', which will only get in the way. But tackle critical 'complexity' that must be resolved. It is important to be able to tell the difference.

Customers are looking for simple intuitive solutions

The simplest solution is usually the best

Cultivate clean, lean and agile thinking

Deliver elegant customer solutions

Work through your processes and cut out any confusion or irrelevance. Focus on providing simple customer friendly solutions not over-engineered complexities.

Look at every element of what you do and ask yourself whether you have opted for the simplest solution.

Apply Occam's Razor

Occam's Razor tells us that, *'All things being equal, the simplest solution is usually the best.'*

So if you turn on a light switch, and there is no light assume that the bulb has gone. But if you turn on the switch in another room and again there is no light, assume that there is a problem with the circuit breaker. Why? Because the circuit breaker being faulty is more likely than two bulbs independently going at exactly the same time.

Applying this to business, let's say that typically you get 100 website enquiries a day and overnight this drops to zero. Here, first check this out with your website hosting company before assuming there's been a sudden drop in demand for your product or service!

Less is more

It's important not to overload the customer with unnecessary layers of complexity or choice. A pushy market trader keen to make a sale will foist upon you 20 or more different types of jewellery, whereas the exclusive upmarket Bond Street jeweller will just display three elegant pieces of jewellery in their shop window.

Keep it intuitive

Today customers expect to be able to instantly and intuitively understand how to use a product or service they have purchased. If they're buying a board game, they're going to open the box, get out the board and start rolling the dice. They're not going to read complicated instructions on how to play the game. (They may check out a few rules later as they progress.)

Einstein said, *'If you can't explain it to a six-year-old, you don't understand it yourself.'*

So make sure everything passes Einstein's six-year-old test. If the answer is No, then you're probably over complicating things and do not have an elegant simple solution.

Engage with simplicity

Simplicity allows you to cut through to the key message. It's a great way to get immediate engagement with your target audience.

Let's take a garden designer seeking to stand out in their marketplace.

Simplicity is recognising that most people simply want their garden transformed. They are not interested in you laboriously explaining the technicalities of the process.

So instead why not produce a one minute time-lapse video of a similar type of garden being transformed from a junk yard to a breathtaking outside space.

Apply lean thinking

Lean thinking is a process of improving the effectiveness and efficiency of a business process by eliminating or revamping activities that do not add value to the customer or your organisation.

In practical terms it means carefully working through your systems and processes to check for any duplication, over-complication, unnecessary activities, cumbersome or muddled sequencing, confusing labelling and over-engineered superfluous elements.

Toyota pioneered this approach and McDonald's is an excellent example of lean thinking in practice, as is Disney.

Disney cuts the queues

A specific example of lean thinking would be Disney's Splash Mountain ride. Customers were dissatisfied about queueing, and slow customer throughput was also affecting Disney's profits.

Disney came up with the idea of people boarding the boat from one side and exiting the boat from the other. A simple lean solution.

You could be applying the same thinking to every process in your own business.

McDonald's – improving every day since 1948

McDonald's is always reviewing the whole process of serving a customer, including how best to take an order, deal with the payment, organise the food preparation and deliver the order to the customer.

This includes thinking about pre-preparing food ingredients for popular orders, whilst also producing the minimum of waste and constantly reviewing what is the fastest service process for the customer.

This practice of identifying the most expedient process continues now with the new automated ordering service.

Apply the KIS principle – Keep-Improve-Stop

A simple practical technique is to look at each element of your own process and ask whether it should be kept, whether it could be improved, or whether you should stop (or eliminate) this from the process.

Apply clean thinking

Steve Jobs introduced us to the 'clean thinking' concept with his comment: *'Simple can be harder than complex. You have to work hard to get your thinking clean to make it simple. But it's worth it in the end because once you get there, you can move mountains.'*

There are many dimensions to cultivating clean thinking. But an important one is how you initially frame a problem. You're unlikely to come up with a simple solution to a problem if you haven't first fully defined – crystallised – the problem you're solving.

Illustration: Flying on a wing and a prayer

Let's take a wartime example of planes returning from a mission with damage from anti-aircraft fire. The damage was analysed, and a decision taken to reinforce the areas of the plane that had been hit by enemy fire.

But here a 'clean thinker' in the team made the point that planes with this type of damage had managed to survive. So it was suggested that instead they should get information on the planes that had been shot down and identify the kind of damage they had sustained.

Reinforcing the damaged parts of the planes that were the cause of them crashing would lessen the vulnerability of this type of plane. This would be a better preventative measure before the next sortie than reinforcing the damaged areas of planes that had at least managed to limp home.

Apply agile thinking

Agile thinking supports the goal of simplicity because it helps us identify unnecessary work that should not be done!

This type of thinking is about setting up pragmatic ways of working that revolve around motivated individuals being allowed to work in a conducive environment with the support they need. It is about trusting people to get the job done in a flexible way.

This is in contrast to relying on there being formalised overly rigid frameworks, methodologies and contracts to determine how that task should be done.

Thus, in the past, products may be launched with a classic 'stage gate' process whereby a series of boxes have to be ticked as the product progresses through different formalised stages.

Today, organisations may set up a 'scrum team' focusing on tasks to be undertaken in short 'sprints' by highly motivated individuals who have the autonomy and freedom to decide how to deliver priority outcomes.

We know that these days multinationals, that normally would take a year or more to launch a new brand of say bottled mineral water, can now – with agile thinking – go from initial idea to launch in a few months!

Optimise your resources

We've established that strategic entrepreneurs know where to play in the marketplace and know how to win by focusing on what matters most.

But in addition critically they will also get there by using the minimum of resources. By this we mean that they will pinpoint the fastest route to securing paying customers and sidestep inefficient processes and time and money sinks.

Employ the minimum viable product (MVP) principle

Let's look at a concrete technique for bringing together much of what we've been saying about identifying elegant solutions, applying lean, clean and agile thinking whilst using the least resources. This is the minimum viable product approach.

The minimum viable product is the intersection between...

○ An ultra-simple version of a product that solves the customer's problem in the simplest way possible, without any extra frills.

And...

○ What is initially practicable in terms of the creation and delivery of the product/service from the organisation's standpoint.

It's a process that reflects the *build the plane as you fly it* principle we referred to earlier. Below we provide a quick overview of the key stages.

An overview of the MVP process

There are essentially four stages to the MVP process. Let's explain each by taking an illustration of introducing a monitor to help people reduce their energy bills.

One: Identify all the critical assumptions made in developing your idea

Let's assume that the first critical assumption is that our target customer is a university educated male, aged 35 to 50, living in an inner city who is prepared to spend a premium price of £360 for our product.

We also assumed that he will be looking for a product that provides continuous data readings on energy consumption in each room, and has easy-to-read displays, coupled with the provision of daily tips on how to reduce energy consumption delivered to a mobile app.

Two: Prioritise the most critical assumption

Next, in the MVP process is pinpointing the one key assumption that seems to be most critical to success.

Let's say in our example that this is the fact that our target customer is willing to pay £360 and that the top benefit sought is receiving specific tips on how to reduce energy consumption.

The point being, if we get this critical assumption wrong, then the whole business model falls apart.

Three: Build an MVP to validate this critical assumption

Now we could rigorously test this most critical assumption by setting up a basic website that promotes the product at a price of £360 and dials up our distinctive benefit of providing regular tips on energy saving.

Four: Launch and adapt

We are now in a position to start building the optimum product out of the rolling, incoming feedback we have received from the customers who have visited the embryonic website we have set up.

Here, by checking how many customers we have generated, and listening to the feedback provided, we can now adjust the offer and adapt our marketing and pricing strategy accordingly and progress.

Interestingly Zappos essentially followed this process in order to determine whether it was viable to start selling shoes *online*.

Before it built the infrastructure to sell shoes online it simply set up a website with photos taken of a selection of shoes to assess interest in the concept. At this point, it just sourced the footwear from regular outlets and despatched them in the post.

Only once it knew this idea had legs, did it commit to investing in the full organisational infrastructure needed to underpin an online shoe business.

Simplicity is good for business

Simplicity will help you when it comes to making your idea happen.

Being able to provide elegant and simple not cumbersome and confused solutions will deliver massive benefits to your business.

In today's often confused, fast moving and complicated world customers will welcome products and services that are simple and straightforward.

Finding simple lean ways of delivering your product or service will help your own business to thrive and stay competitive.

Key actions

✓ In working towards providing simple solutions for your customers, apply clean thinking at the outset to make sure you're working on the core problem.

✓ Put your processes through a lean and agile thinking process in order to ensure you're not providing over-engineered products and/or services.

✓ Consider using the minimum viable product approach as a way of identifying what are the most critical factors you need to get right first, before developing a full product or service.

→ *Entrepreneurs know that 'All things being equal, the simplest solution is usually the best'.*

12: APPLY BUSINESS ACUMEN
Highlights

Be clear on your business model

Getting total clarity around your business model may seem **common sense**, but it is not often common practice.

Take time to **get on top of the numbers**. Without having total clarity around your cost structure in relation to revenue, you will run into difficulty.

Many businesses fail because they don't ever get to grips with their **key metrics** – their gross margin and likely net profit.

Focus on the value you provide

Price your offer around the **value you are providing** - not just based on your supply costs. Don't fall into the trap of being an undervalued commodity.

Focus on the value you are generating. Avoid a race to the bottom on price. **Give out a value, not low-cost, vibe.**

By demonstrating the value you provide you will be **creating demand** rather than chasing it.

Go for premium pricing

Go for a premium pricing policy based on the added value you are providing. Know where you fit relative to **key competitive price points**.

Start by establishing the cost to the customer if they were to undertake this work themselves - the **DIY** cost!

Then determine what a near **competitor** with a similar cost base to your own typically charges.

Then get clear on what is the **'Rolls Royce'** top price - what the most successful company in your sector is charging.

Then be bold - go for a price towards the **top end of the range**.

CREATIVITY AND NUMBERS: Begin to think of business as being a combination of creative marketing and mathematics

Apply business acumen

Luck is not a business model.

Anthony Bourdain

Many creative entrepreneurs with great ideas fail because they do not get their head around the business realities. So, it is important to know how you will monetise your idea.

Apply sound business judgement and acumen to ensure you have a viable and profitable business. This may sound obvious – common sense. But it is not always common practice.

Get total clarity around your business model (and how you will monetise your idea)

Focus on the value you provide not the cost of your services

Develop a system for generating profitable customers

Ensure you have a sound business model

Amazingly, many people embark on their entrepreneurial journey without putting in the fundamental thinking about their business model. You need to have total clarity around exactly how you will monetise your idea.

A sound business model requires you to have:

- ○ An accurate picture of your infrastructure and overhead costs.

- ○ A detailed itemisation of the costs of supplying your product or service.

- ○ A well-thought-through pricing strategy: one that will generate the required gross margin and targeted profit levels.

- A realistic assessment of likely sales – one that is not based on 'fantasy' forecasts, but on an informed assessment of the likely take up of your idea.

- Factored in payment for your time at a reasonable market rate (wage) rather than ignoring this and running the business on thin air.

Stay grounded in business reality not fantasy

The excitement of setting up a new business can lead some entrepreneurs to let their heart rule their head. They start making decisions based on emotion not reason. Let's look at some watch outs.

- Investing in office premises, equipment and kit <u>ahead</u> of securing the revenue needed to pay for this.

- Being tempted to undertake expensive longer term marketing and branding exercises rather than focusing on immediate strategies to generate concrete sales in the short term.

- Developing fantasy sales forecasts about possible future work. Remember forecasts are essentially made up!

- Failing to understand the difference between good and bad debt. Bad debt would be borrowing money to spend on initiatives such as lavish office refurbishment that don't have an immediate impact on the bottom line. Good debt is, for example, investing in £X in Google ads, if you know from experience that you are almost guaranteed to receive 10 times this in return by way of sales.

- Omitting to cost into projects and initiatives, the amount of time you are spending on a project. This leads to a false sense of whether you are making a profit. You need to be aware that your time has an opportunity cost.

- Being tempted by vanity and ego projects such as running an industry event on a pro-bono basis. Networking can be good, but you've got to ensure that these activities don't lead you to take your eye off the ball.

- o Chasing revenue because a big number looks good but, in achieving this, falling into the trap of taking on projects that are not profitable.

- o Learning to say no to the 'crazy makers' who are tempting you into projects you know are just not going to make money. You need the confidence to start saying no rather than saying yes in an anxiety to please.

In sum, winning entrepreneurs ensure that business *nous* triumphs over ego, make believe and fantasy. They have their heads screwed on when it comes to knowing the critical business metrics.

Know your key business numbers

In order to build a sound business model, one that's based in reality not fantasy, you need to apply clear, accurate thinking to pinpoint the key business metrics. Do not just rely on fantasy estimates or wishful thinking.

Don't worry about having exact information. B*ack of an envelope* calculations using the best easily available information is a helpful start point. Some key metrics are reviewed below.

Your gross margin

One critical key number that you must pin down in building your entrepreneurial venture is your gross margin.

Gross margin is the difference between your revenue and the cost of supplying your product/service, divided by revenue. Gross margin is often expressed as a percentage. So, it is the selling price of an item, less the cost of producing/acquiring the item.

Total clarity on what gross margin you need to make your business viable is essential.

Gross and net profit

With a firm handle on your gross margin, you will then need have clarity on two further critical numbers. These are:

○ *Gross profit* is your profit after deducting your cost of sales (the costs associated with making and selling your product, or the costs associated with providing your service).

○ *Net profit* is your sales income (revenue) minus all your business costs including your cost of sales plus overheads such as wages, office costs, IT etc.)

The cost of acquiring a customer

It is helpful to know the cost of acquiring a customer (say through Google Ads or Facebook Ads). It's also helpful to know the lifetime value of your customers.

The profitability of customers

Be clear on the profitability of different categories of customer: the revenue they bring you and their cost to you.

Operating cashflow

A massive problem for entrepreneurs and small business owners is managing their cashflow. This is not about overall levels of sales and profit but about knowing you have cash available to keep the show on the road.

Specifically this means knowing your average debtor days – that is what is the time delay before you're actually paid. Your terms may be 30 days but these days many small businesses find they only get paid after around 90 days – maybe even longer!

Get your pricing right

As a generalisation many entrepreneurs, freelancers and small business owners do not charge a sufficiently high enough price. They get nervous about losing business and let their profit margins drift downwards. Here you need the confidence to charge for the value you are providing rather than being driven into a commodity market.

Focus on the value you're providing

Set your price based on the benefits and transformational value you're providing for customers. Do not price just based on covering costs and adding a margin.

Do not fall into the trap of being an undervalued 'commodity'. You need to avoid a race to the bottom on price. Get paid not simply for the work you do and the time you put in, but for who you are and the value you create. The endgame is to avoid being an interchangeable commodity that sells based on price.

Send out the vibe that you are providing tremendous value for money. In this way you will naturally attract customers to you.

Do not be that less confident person who feels they need to sell their product or service solely on price.

Be confident about going for a premium price

People will pay a premium price for the right product and service. So, build the confidence to price based on the value you provide. Do not end up undercharging. If you are providing transformational value and eliminating risk and uncertainty for customers, they will pay.

In setting your price look at three perspectives

Look at price from the following perspectives. This will help you to arrive at the optimum price point for your offer – one that is towards the top end of the pricing range.

- Have an idea of what the cost to the client would be if they were to undertake this work for themselves on a *DIY basis*.

- Be clear on what a *near competitor* with a similar cost base to you might charge.

- Pinpoint the *top end of the range premium prices* – what your leading most successful competitors would charge.

Price justification

Sometimes it is helpful to provide a 'price justification' – the context to your price. If and when appropriate, set out the time and resources that have gone into you shaping your product or service offer.

This will help the buyer set your price in some kind of context and remind them of the cost they would incur if they had to create for themselves what you are offering.

So, if you are providing an organic food product there could be merit in explaining the way this is nurtured and cultivated so as to justify the higher price being charged compared to a non-organic version.

Know how to negotiate

Another dimension to building your business acumen is having the confidence and skills to negotiate an appropriate deal. This could be around negotiating with suppliers about the costs of securing key components and services and/or about how you negotiate a price with a stakeholder or potential customer. Below we provide some guidance on arriving at an optimum outcome.

Focus on principles not personalities

Move the discussion away from personalities towards focusing on the fundamental goals of the negotiation. Do not classify someone as being a friend or an adversary. Think of them as fellow problem solvers.

Avoid the negotiation being a contest of wills

Shift the agenda away from one party 'making demands' and the other party then needing to 'make concessions'.

Frame the negotiation around stakeholders being prepared to listen to compelling fundamental principles. Do not make the negotiation as being about individuals having to yield under undue pressure.

Do not focus on red line positions

Move away from the idea of there being non-negotiable red line positions that must be defended at all costs. Instead work to identify areas of emerging agreement that can be refined and developed.

Develop options for mutual gain

Do not get locked into the idea of there being only one single answer that everyone must accept but move towards the notion of there being multiple options for consideration.

Do not position the negotiation task as being about victory or loss. Instead position this as both parties working towards a mutually beneficial goal.

Take care with your language

Move the language away from talking about people who you '*trust*' or '*distrust*'. Instead, use language that builds trust in all parties – language that focuses on the mutual interest in solving the common problem.

Develop the Third Corner perspective

Look at issues from the outside-in – third corner – perspective. This will encourage you to identify the key concepts in play. This is about identifying the main principle or concept at the core of what is being negotiated.

This will help to depersonalise differing points of view. This approach will minimise the chances of you becoming embroiled in unhelpful win/lose personality conflicts.

Let's take an illustration away from business. Let's say you are in a passionate discussion about the merits or otherwise of private education. Here, you can take the heat out of any conflict by focusing on the key concepts in place. So, why not focus on the two (arguably) equally honourable principles – concepts – in play here. These are 'freedom of choice' (in how to spend one's money) and 'equal opportunity' in education.

Build a marketing system

A lot of small businesses suffer from feast and famine. They do some marketing and attract some customers. But then become so overwhelmed with getting the work done that they don't devote sufficient time to securing the next tranche of customers or business.

Here it's helpful to think about how to build a system for the *'rhythmic generation'* of customers, sales and profits.

The ideal is to have steady *deal flow*. By this we mean always having in the pipeline a flow of potential customers. So what does this mean in practical terms?

The start point for achieving this is to recognise that 'marketing what you do' is perhaps more important than 'doing what you do'. So carve out one hour a day (minimum) that you dedicate to marketing and securing that *deal flow*.

Underpin your actions with business acumen

Often the business model underpinning a venture is given insufficient attention. Business owners get carried away with the excitement of setting up their business and creating a new brand but ignore critical factors, such as the gross margin required to keep their business viable.

Business common sense goes out of the window and they engage in wishful thinking about how to monetise their idea.

Fantasy sets in about possible sales that may be just around the corner, but these are often no more than a pipedream.

So it is critical that if you want to turn your idea into action then you must stay anchored and grounded in the business realities.

By all means think big. But constantly ask questions about the practical side of things. Know your key numbers and focus on the value you are providing – thereby opening the door to charging a premium price.

Key actions

✓ Critically review your business model to make sure it's grounded in reality and not built out of fantasy and wishful thinking.

✓ Make sure you have total mastery of the key metrics you need to know in order to run a profitable business. Making sure you hit your gross margin target is critical.

✓ Work on creating demand for your services by focusing on the transformational value you provide, rather than getting trapped into a commodity market where you're always selling on price.

(→) *Get total clarity around your business model. This may seem common sense, but it is often not common practice.*

PART FOUR: APPLY CLEAR THINKING
Recap

Embrace strategic excellence

We started by looking at how successful entrepreneurs think clearly and accurately before they act. This is the golden thread that runs through their success. Applying clear thinking seems obvious but many business owners start with good intentions but then quickly get overwhelmed with day to day firefighting. Amidst all this hassle they fail to take time out for clear deep thinking.

A critical area where clear thinking is required is in ensuring you are in a sound strategic place. It is an uphill battle if you are operating with a flawed business strategy.

If you wanted an inspirational illustration of strategic thinking in action, look at Reid Hoffman, the founder of LinkedIn. He spotted a gap in the market for a system that would facilitate professional networking and help people build their careers. It was this clarity of strategic thinking that paved the way for subsequent success.

Provide simple solutions

The next area we examined was applying clear thinking to providing simple uncomplicated solutions. Here the stories of Steve Jobs' endless pursuit of simplicity – the hallmark of Apple's success – are legendary. My favourite is, in pursuit of designing an even thinner iPad, Jobs dropping a prototype into an office fish tank and saying, 'you can do better... those bubbles represent wasted space'.

Apply business acumen

Finally, in looking at clear thinking we stressed the importance of applying this to the development of a winning business model. For inspiration look at the way Jeff Bezos built Amazon around a fundamentally simple, but highly effective business model. He knew what would work – build an ever broader selection of products, keep the pricing competitive and invest in ever faster delivery.

PART FIVE: BE DIFFERENT
Overview

The difficulty lies not so much in developing new ideas as in escaping from old ones.

John Maynard Keynes

13. Add creative edge

A key dimension in making ideas happen is to focus on being different. This is important in today's crowded marketplace where you need to stand out and make sure your voice is heard.

The starting point for this, which we look at in the opening chapter of this part of the book, is to see what extra edge of creativity – different thinking – you can bring to your venture. What innovations, enhancements and points of difference can you bring to your idea by digging deep into your creative self.

14. Touch their world

In this chapter we look at a massive source of inspiration for creative ideas. This is understanding in depth your customers' needs: 'touching their world'. It is critical that you are totally customer centric in everything you do. This depth of understanding – almost an ability to empathise with your customers and stakeholders – will help you build a competitive advantage. This will help you ensure your ideas happen.

15. Showcase your difference

And in the final chapter in this part of the book we look at ways in which you can showcase the points of difference that distinguish your product or service from others. It is about drawing out why you are different and being able to explain this clearly, succinctly and memorably to your customers and stakeholders.

13: ADD CREATIVE EDGE

Highlights

Creativity is a big differentiator

The ability to **think differently** and imaginatively drives entrepreneurial success.

Always **add creative flair** to differentiate yourself from the competition.

Your ability to **innovate** and be different will pay massive dividends.

Believe you are creative

Break out of any limitations and unleash your creative self.
Believe you can '**make your own kind of music**'.

Believe that your creativity can be **cultivated** and enhanced.

Creativity is a very disciplined business - it doesn't just drift down from the muse in some mysterious way. So you need to **work at it**.

Solve problems with creativity

In the business context much **creativity is about solving a problem** - rather than being a kind of magical ability.

So, focus on solving **customer pain points** in a creative way.

Provide those little product and/or service extras that will **excite and delight** your customers.

THE WOW FACTOR: Focus on finding the emotional hooks that will attract customers to your offer

Add creative edge

Creativity is a very disciplined business.

Attributed to Julie Andrews

The ability to think differently and imaginatively defines entrepreneurial success. The good news is that creativity does not just drift down from the muse in some mysterious way. It's possible to cultivate and enhance your creativity. There are simple techniques to help you provide that creative edge to your entrepreneurial venture.

Creativity is a massive differentiator that will drive your competitive advantage

Creativity can be cultivated

Be a renegade thinker who is always thinking outside the box to provide creative customer solutions

Believe in your inner creativity

The start point for developing your creativity is to break out of any limitations you have about your ability to be creative. Unleash your creative self by recognising that creativity comes in many different forms.

From the business perspective it's helpful to think of creativity as a form of problem solving, rather than being some mystical magical act.

Barnes Wallis the inventor is reputed as saying, *'I've never invented anything. All I've done is respond to problems.'*

And Johnny Mercer the songwriter when asked, *'What comes first? The words or the music?'* apparently replied pragmatically, *'The phone call'*!

Deepak Chopra reminds us that, *'Solving problems should be a joy, a welcome challenge to our creativity.'*

115

A framework for boosting creativity

The creative process is a combination of imagination and reason. The outputs of our imagination are modified by our rational thinking. At the same time our rational thinking can be bent into new shapes through imaginative thought. It is this fusion of the left brain (logical) and right brain (creative) ways of thinking about a problem that can trigger creative ideas.

Everyone's approach to creativity will be different, but the following framework may help you develop your own personal creativity 'system'.

Be in a creative surrounding

Select an environment that will maximise your chances of getting into the creative zone and encourage the creative juices to flow. Pick locations that will help you get into the creative flow.

Immerse yourself in the challenge

Make sure you immerse yourself in the context to, and details of, the problem under investigation. Be totally clear on all the moving parts of the problem you are trying to understand: what is *known* and what is *unknown*.

Set boundaries and precisely frame the creative challenge

Setting boundaries can enhance creative thinking because it provides a clear focus for imaginative thought. We touched on this earlier. So, for example, setting the general goal of 'improving the creativity of your website' is likely to be less effective than focusing in on the <u>specific</u> goal of 'giving your homepage a hook that will stimulate visitors to lean in and check out your offer.'

Sleep on it

Another idea is to let the subconscious do its job. We referred earlier to Stephen King thinking about his initial ideas overnight. And Julia Cameron, the writer, talks about 'asking for an answer in the <u>evening</u> and listening for the answer in <u>morning</u>.'

Apply divergent and convergent modes of thinking

Bringing different styles of thinking to the process helps trigger creative solutions. These include:

Convergent thinking – this is more linear, focused and systematic in its approach.

Divergent thinking – this moves outwards, producing lots of ideas but not necessarily in a logical order. It helps us navigate ambiguity and review a wide range of possible, often risky, possibilities.

An illustration

Let's say we want to make business meetings more productive, enjoyable and effective.

- ○ *Convergent thinking* would take us to examining the skills and expertise of the chairperson, how the agenda is organised and how the room is laid out, and so on.

- ○ *Divergent thinking* may challenge the fundamental meeting concept and come up with the idea of, for instance, 'walking meetings' whereby teams tackle a topic whilst on the move, rotating who is talking to whom during the walk!

Co-create: involve others

There are numerous techniques that help stimulate creativity that involve working creatively with others.

For example there is *brainstorming* of which there are different variations. But essentially this is about encouraging people, free from constraints, to throw out their ideas in a spontaneous free-flowing way.

These ideas can then be shared with others who, in a non-judgemental or evaluative way, build on these and generate further ideas. Then the process concludes with an overall collective assessment of which ideas might be taken forward.

A further idea is to *seek out sounding boards* and invite constructive critique. Securing feedback on your initial creative ideas can be very enriching. Even the greats such as TS Eliot did this. Apparently *The Wasteland* benefitted massively from constructive critique by Ezra Pound.

The use of creativity techniques

There are a host of techniques in the toolbag to help us think creatively. One I particularly like is the way Brian Eno, who most notably collaborated with David Bowie, used *oblique strategies* to prompt and take even someone as creative as Bowie to the next level.

In essence this involves randomly selecting from a box of cards different 'challenging constraints' with the aim of breaking any creative blocks and encouraging lateral thinking.

Each card contains a suggestion or remark aimed at breaking a deadlock or a dilemma that could be blocking a musical composition.

These prompts could include: 'use an old idea'; 'what can you reduce'; 'what would your closest friend do?' through to 'work at a different speed.' The cards also embraced complex ideas such as 'accept what may be perceived as an error as a hidden intention that it should be included'.

The light bulb 'aha' moment

Finally you need to know when you've reached a point in the creative process when there are no further gains to be made from continuing to work on the problem. You've arrived at the optimum imaginative, innovative solution.

Foster creativity by seeking out the big concepts

One specific technique for arriving at a creative innovative solution is to pinpoint the bigger picture concepts and principles in play around the product or service you are considering introducing.

The Starbucks 'third place' concept

An illustration of creativity flowing from thinking about bigger concepts is the creation of Starbucks. They looked at the fundamental positioning of coffee shops and challenged this with a new concept.

The Starbucks analysis led them to the notion of people wanting a 'third place' in their lives, somewhere between their work and their home.

Once Starbucks recognised that people were looking for a place to relax, use their laptop and not just grab a cup of coffee and run, then you have the idea – concept – of positioning your chain of coffee shops as a third place – somewhere between work and home.

Be a renegade

Another way of prompting your creativity is to get into 'renegade' mode. Be that person who challenges cherished beliefs and standard industry norms rather than simply defaulting to the way things are always done.

Avoid the *'this is how we have always done things round here'* syndrome. For example, for many decades professional services, such as lawyers, accountants and dentists, resisted any form of marketing that was commonplace in other industry sectors, on the grounds that this was inappropriate.

But then some organisations broke ranks and started overtly marketing their services and now quite sophisticated marketing is typical of many professional services.

Add a twist of originality

Another dimension to providing that creative edge is to just add a small twist of originality to quite traditional ways of doing things. Below we have provided three illustrations of this idea in action.

Targeted leaflet drops

A local garage prepared different *We offer MOTs for your car* leaflets for all of the major brands they covered – Ford, Volvo, Mercedes etc.

Then on a Sunday morning – knowing that this is when cars would be parked outside customers' houses – they put a bespoke *car brand specific* promotional leaflet in each letterbox.

Live stream your flower preparation

If you own a flower shop, why not video the preparation of a customer's gift order and send this to the person receiving the flowers.

Podcasts on gardening

Your garden centre may not have a better choice of products or have lower prices. But introducing inspiring and informed weekly podcasts with gardening tips could be a conversation starter – your point of difference.

Adapt ideas from others – success leaves clues

A further technique for stimulating creativity is to see what you can learn from the success of those in other sectors.

For example, accident and emergency paramedic teams benefitted from studies of how Formula One racing teams were able to change the wheels on racing cars, and undertake other running repairs, during the seven seconds or so that a car comes into the pits.

They learned that the F1 mechanics anticipated all the likely problem scenarios that the F1 driver might have, so that when he pulled into the pit lane, they were pre-prepared with the tools and parts. They were ready to solve that particular problem.

So, the idea of anticipating problems and being prepared with instant solutions was incorporated into how emergency services organise and create pre-prepared medical kits for the different health and accident scenarios they may encounter.

Creativity is today's big differentiator

When we are talking about adding a creative edge, we do not necessarily mean coming up with a completely different hitherto never been introduced idea. If you can do this all well and good. But as a minimum you need to make sure that there is some point of difference that distinguishes your offer.

The key is to open yourself up to exploring your own creative potential. For many their creativity gets closed down early in the education system and they get into a conformity mode of thinking where they simply follow the herd.

The more creative route is to experiment with your play instinct. So relax into looking for those points of difference – that innovative dimension – you can add to help push up the probability of your idea happening.

Putting that extra dimension of forensic creative energy into pinpointing a standout point of difference is crucial to ensuring your idea gets airtime in today's highly competitive environment.

Key actions

✓ Believe in your ability to cultivate your creativity. Some are more naturally creative than others. But everyone can go to the next level by applying themselves to come up with creative ideas.

✓ Make your default position one that is always trying to be different rather than blindly following the herd.

✓ Devise your own system or process or framework for maximising your own ability to come up with creative ideas. Don't just leave this to chance. Creativity is a very disciplined business.

→ *Unleash your creative self. Break out of any limitations. Believe you can!*

14. TOUCH THEIR WORLD
Highlights

Know what makes your customers tick

An obsession with your customers is essential if you want to succeed as an entrepreneur. It's **often the little things that make the biggest difference.**

Develop a deep-seated understanding of what is really important to your customers. **Know what really motivates them** - tap into their emotions.

Be honest with yourself about how well your systems cope with different types of customer. Are you working hard enough to make them **enjoyable, simple, intuitive and easy to follow?**

Listen to what customers are saying

Successful entrepreneurs constantly **ask their customers questions** – **and listen**. Then they turn this insight into a competitive advantage.

Identify the key **customer touchpoints** and learn from role playing being the customer from hell!

Ask yourself whether you are **creating a memorable experience** at each customer touchpoint.

See things as they are

See your business **through the lens of the customer**, not through rose tinted glasses! See it as it is - not as you would like it to be.

Exceed your customers' expectations. Surprise them by **going the extra mile**.

Always **take fast remedial action** if you sense any disconnect with what customers want and what you provide.

ASK YOURSELF: How easy is it for customers to do business with me – is it effortless or more like getting behind enemy lines?

Touch their world

Whatever you do, do it well. Do it so well that when people see you do it, they will want to come back and see you do it again, and they will want to bring others and show them how well you do what you do.

Walt Disney

Listening to your customers and being customer centric is vital in making your business different. This comes down to asking customers questions and turning this feedback – knowledge – into first class customer service. This can be an outstanding point of competitive advantage.

It's about putting the customer at the centre of your business and developing a deep-seated understanding of what is important to them.

This focus on customers – knowing what is important to them and responding to their needs – sets you apart from your competitors.

Think from your customers' perspective

Know what makes your customers tick

Be genuinely committed to customer centricity

Take the outside-in customer perspective

Think *outside-in* from the customer's perspective – not *inside-out* from the standpoint of your own systems and processes. Ensure you see things as they are – not through rose tinted glasses as you would like them to be. It's about what customers expect, not what's convenient for your business.

Find out what delights and excites your customers, identify what annoys or frustrates them, and find out what's missing or absent in your product or service offer. If you sense any disconnect between your offer and your customer's needs, you should take fast appropriate remedial action.

Identify the core benefit motivating customers

In touching your customer's world focus on the 'benefits' you offer not just the features you provide. Some small business owners are often so proud of their product's *features* that they forget to highlight the customer *benefits* they are offering.

They focus too much on the detailed features and not enough on the emotional benefits they are offering – the motivational transformational experience they are providing.

Many know the classic drill-bit example used to explain the difference between customers' wants and emotional needs. The customer may <u>ask</u> for a drill-bit but <u>want</u> a small hole to go on the wall to insert a picture hook. But, going beyond this, what they really <u>need</u> is the pleasure of seeing a picture of their grandchildren on the wall each day.

So, focus on the end transformational outcome, not just on the features and/or technical process.

Let's illustrate this point with a couple of examples.

Illustration: How Lego refocused on its key success driver

Even the big successful companies can take their eye off the ball and drift away from what it is that really drives their success. Let's take Lego, their sales plateaued. They were just continuing to offer more kinds of kits that kids could assemble.

They then, through customer research, secured the insight that their core success driver was their understanding of the concept of *play*.

Lego was the company that 'owned' and understood play better than anyone else in the children's toy market. Generations of kids had been playing with Lego with stories being handed down from grandparents and parents to children since the company was founded in 1932.

This insight refocused Lego on encouraging kids to build models from their own imagination. This led to the *Lego Movie* theme that reinforced Lego's *mission* of '**inspiring and developing the builders of tomorrow**' and its *vision* of '**inventing the future of play**'.

Illustration: From selling apartments to being in the business of moving lives

Let's take another example of the importance of focusing on the core phenomenon at the heart of a challenge. This is a property company that had built elegant looking apartments which were designed for downsizing buyers - people moving from bigger houses as they got older to live in smaller accommodation. However, they found that sales were sluggish.

Initially they thought the problem was the design of the apartments. But what this company eventually established was that design wasn't the problem.

The reason for resistance to purchase shown by downsizers was the trouble they were having adjusting to a new mode of living. If they bought an apartment, they wouldn't be able to entertain the whole family for Christmas lunch.

The solution to boosting sales lay not around redesigning the apartments, but about going into the business of helping people **psychologically make the transition from one life stage to another.**

So, the property company repositioned itself as supporting customers during this stage of their lives: it recognised it was in the *moving lives* not just property business. They had discovered what would really motivate people to buy and enjoy their apartments.

Listen, learn and act

Listening will give you a better understanding of your customer's world. But you need not only to listen to your customers but also take action based on this.

We hear a lot about the importance of being a 'good listener', but often without thinking through exactly what this means.

Listening is partly about the mental discipline of paying attention – putting the focus on the other person – not yourself, and carefully listening to what they have to say.

But being a good listener is more than just listening. It is also about how you then act. It's about how you will intelligently link what you have *learnt* from your listening to the next action you will take. It's about what action flows from your act of listening.

And being a good listener does not end here – with following through with action. It also includes, based on your listening, reflecting on how this is influencing your view of the world.

Is your listening prompting you to start asking yourself whether – through genuinely listening to others – you now wish to change your outlook, agenda, or behaviour.

For example, after intently listening to someone telling you what it is like to have become homeless, this might just prompt you to revisit your beliefs and value-set around this topic.

Work at unearthing powerful customer insights

We have established that identifying powerful insights about what motivates your customers will help you fashion a distinctive offer.

Building a deep understanding of what is truly driving customers – tapping into what makes them really tick – will serve you well in being able to touch your customer's world.

However here it is important to be clear on what we mean by an 'insight'. A true insight will take you into what is behind a dilemma or tension with which a customer is grappling. This will open up opportunities to provide solutions that touch their world.

Specifically a true insight has two critical dimensions:

- o **A psychological dimension:** describes what is inside the customer's mind – their causal motivations, attitudes, beliefs and feelings.

- o **A behavioural dimension:** describes what is observable – what the customer is or is not doing as a result of these causal and psychological factors.

126

For example, once you've had the 'insight' that many dog owners think of their dogs as their 'children' – one of the family – then this could inspire you to be creative in the way you set up your offer to, and marketing communications with, dog owners.

Seek out customer feedback

By talking to a mix of your current and potential customers you will get some great insights about how you can sharpen your offer – make it more *irresistible*.

Set up a dialogue with customers to give you the outside-in perspective

Thomas Berger said, *'The art and science of asking questions is the source of all knowledge.'* So keep asking powerful and penetrating questions about your customers' experience.

As we touched on earlier, there are lots of simple, easy to implement customer research techniques that will help you better understand your customers.

Ask about what would transform the customer experience

My go-to question to understand how to improve a product or service is:

If you had a magic wand what one single change or improvement would you make to the product and or service we provide?

This is a very powerful way of identifying and then improving any particular shortcoming or limitations to your product or service.

Focus on the pain points

Another lens through which to understand your customers is to explore the problems or pain points they may be facing. If you understand and address these you will get instant lean-in. Customers will recognise that you are on their side.

Pinpoint the fundamental change the customer is seeking

When coaching, a question I will often ask to pinpoint the core challenge facing a business owner is, *'What is* not *true now that has to be true at the end of our coaching session for you to believe that you have received value from me as a coach?'*

So if the business owner says that it is not true that *'I'm a really confident presenter'* then I know to zero in on this challenge and start making this a 'true statement' by the end of my coaching.

Role play being the customer from hell

One suggestion is to role play, and learn from, being the *customer from hell:* critically review your performance from this perspective!

Use this feedback to be honest with yourself about how well each of your systems are coping with this type of demanding customer. Are you working hard enough at your product and customer service delivery to make this enjoyable, simple, intuitive and easy to follow?

Ask a critical friend

Another technique for getting the customer perspective on your offer or service is to invite a critical friend – someone whose view you trust and respect – to go through your customer experience and act as a sounding board.

This will provide you with further feedback about where you can make changes that will push up the chances of exceeding your customer or clients' expectations.

Questions to ask a critical friend

Here are some examples of questions you could ask of a critical friend…

What delights and excites you in what we do?

What irritates you about the way we do business?

What is it that most annoys and frustrates you?

Is there anything that is missing or absent in our product or service?

What do you feel we are ignoring and should be paying more attention to?

What does our main competitor do better than us?

If you ran our business what three changes would you make?

Commit to a fantastic customer experience

By developing a laser-like focus on what really motivates your customers, you will be able to create a great customer experience. One specific technique here is to build a profile of your ideal customer (some people call this a customer avatar or persona).

Start by building a profile of your ideal customer: a thumbnail sketch of the personality of the person who you are most ideally suited to serve or provide a product for.

A restaurant example of defining the ideal customer

Tom is the restaurant's ideal customer. He:

- Is willing to pay a premium for quality food.
- Wants exceptional personal service.
- Seeks updates on new dishes.
- Enjoys good conversation and an eating experience that doesn't involve music or noise.
- Is someone they enjoy serving and provides a sound profit margin.

This doesn't mean to say you don't provide excellent service to those outside the ideal customer profile. But having clarity over your ideal customer provides a laser-like focus on what you should consistently be doing particularly well.

Focus on the key customer touchpoints

After creating your customer avatar, identify the 'customer touchpoints' at which you interact with your customers. This starts when the customer first picks up the phone or visits your website or shop.

Then, for each touchpoint ask:

- ○ Are you delivering what your business – brand – is promising?
- ○ Are you proud of the customer experience you have created?
- ○ Are you creating a memorable wow factor at each key touchpoint?
- ○ Are your systems and customer service simple, intuitive and easy to follow?
- ○ Is this experience better than your leading competitors?
- ○ Is there something more you need to do to win them over as repeat customers?
- ○ Are you really going the extra mile? (Everyone senses when they are getting a really great customer experience, rather than being fobbed off.)

So be honest – is what you do really genuinely customer centric or is it really about making the customer fit in your own processes and systems.

Illustration: Who is winning here - the customer or the process?

Scenario Take 1: The customer, looking for a quick bite to eat, arrives at a hotel just a couple of minutes after room service has closed and is told quite emphatically that 'there is nothing that the hotel can do'. *This is an example of the hotel's process winning!*

Scenario Take 2: Here in exactly the same situation, the hotel – although the customer is two minutes late for room service, says 'I'm sure the kitchen can rustle something up'. This *is an example of where customer sovereignty wins over the hotel's internal process.*

Review your own commitment to being truly customer centric

When it comes to touching your customer's world – being genuinely customer centric – it's important to regularly check in with yourself to make sure you have not become complacent.

You need to see things as they really are, not as you'd like them to be. So do not end up seeing the world through rose tinted glasses.

Working for yourself can be a lonely business. So on the one hand, it's a strength to have self-belief in order to sustain yourself through difficult events.

But on the other hand, this shouldn't lead to self-deception about the quality of the product or service you are offering. They say *don't (slavishly) believe your own advertising!*

On the theme of staying genuinely customer centric, here are some questions that you should answer honestly about yourself:

Are you on the same wavelength as your customers – do you really listen to what customers want and genuinely try to solve their problems, rather than focus on your own processes?

Are you ensuring your systems, processes and frontline customer staff consistently deliver your brand promise?

Do you really believe you are doing enough to create a great customer experience?

Do you ever get carried away working on features of your products that are just not important to your customers?

Are you delaying fixing something you know is not right?

Do you regularly rate yourself on your commitment to outstanding customer experience?

Build difference by understanding your customers

The idea of demonstrating that you have understood your customers' needs lies at the heart of your success as an entrepreneur. Some entrepreneurs claim they can do this intuitively, whilst others recognise the value of undertaking market research – setting up a direct dialogue with customers.

But however you achieve this, fully understanding in depth – almost empathising with – the customers' situation is an increasingly important dimension to entrepreneurial success. It will give you a critical point of difference. You will be able to touch your customers' world.

Key actions

✓ Regularly obtain customer feedback and act on this to create a fantastic customer experience.

✓ Focus on the key motivators that really determine why customers will come back to you.

✓ Monitor your commitment to customer centricity to make sure there is no drift from what you think you are doing and what you are actually doing.

> → *See things as they are – not as you would like them to be. See your business through the lens of the customer.*

15: SHOWCASE YOUR DIFFERENCE
Highlights

Don't hide your light under a bushel

Don't shrink from **spelling out** in a forthright way exactly why you're different from your competitors.

No matter how technical, specialist or complex your product or service offering is, it's always possible to **explain to your audience why you're different** in a concise and compelling way.

Be succinct in explaining why you're different

Create a compelling **Elevator Pitch**. Take time out to describe what you do to someone who knows nothing about your business in a few short, punchy and memorable sentences.

Use our **template** to create and refine a powerful Elevator Pitch.

Ensure your website passes the seven-second test

The experts tell us that people initially only spend seven seconds exploring a website to decide **whether the product or service is for them or not**.

So make sure your **website does you justice** and quickly gets over why you're different from your competitors.

ASK YOURSELF: Have I sufficiently differentiated my offer so that it is clear why my customers should buy from me rather than my competitors – have I given them sufficient reason to believe in me?

Showcase your difference

In order to be irreplaceable one must always be different.
Coco Chanel

Getting total clarity around what it is that makes your business different from your competitors is critical. Be confident about telling the world why you are different. Do not hide your light under a bushel.

You need to be able to explain in a few sentences why it is your customers and clients should come to you rather than anyone else.

Communicating why you are different is as important as doing what you do

Differentiate around the transformational benefit you provide

Communicate your difference in a clear, memorable and concise way

Explain your difference with simplicity

We have introduced the 'six-year-old child test' when it comes to explaining things in a simple way. But surprisingly many business owners resist doing this. They fall into the trap of thinking they do not have to do this because they are somehow outside this 'rule'.

Some business owners believe that if there is any justice in the world then the sheer quality and professionalism of what they are doing will somehow magically shine through.

The (mistaken) belief is that you can succeed in business without you having to actively tell the world why you are different. Alas this is not the way the business world works!

You need to dial up – tell the world – why you are different. This seems an obvious maxim. But it seems that certain resistances get in the way of business owners really doing justice to showcasing why they are different.

135

One common resistance is for business owners to believe that their business is a 'special case'. They convince themselves that the nature of their products or services is so intricate or unusual and complicated that it cannot be explained in a few short sentences.

But this is rarely true. Going down the 'we are a special exception to the normal rules of marketing communications' route usually leads to confused messaging. <u>All</u> businesses can showcase their difference in a few short sentences.

Clarify what it is you do and do not want to share

In fashioning effective communications – in showcasing why you are different – reflect on what you need to tell your customers and what it is <u>not</u> necessary to explain.

It's all about having clarity around how you will frame your communication. Below we look at three specific framing issues to get right.

Set the context before getting into the detail

A common error is starting your conversation with the customer by plunging them into too much micro-detail before setting the broader, contextual picture.

So, for example, if you are car wash business, don't start by telling them about a new jet washer with a special power nozzle that you've just purchased. What the customer first needs to know is that you are a car wash business that provides a range of quality, value-for-money services.

Don't tell your audience too much

Then having set out the context and started the process of getting into some detail, do not then fall into the trap of providing unnecessarily detailed information.

You don't want your customers saying, *'why are they telling me all this?'* So you need to ruthlessly self-edit down the essence of what it is you want to say.

So if you are a travel agency, by all means tell them that you have won the Best Travel Agency in the South West of England Award, but they probably don't need to know that you got a grade B in your geography exam at school!

Make explicit to your audience what is implicit to you

Another communications error is not making explicit a particular feature or aspect that is so familiar – implicit – to you that you overlook the need to explain it to an outside audience.

So, you know what the acronym STEM (subjects) means but your customers might not. (STEM: Science, technology, engineering and mathematics.)

Apply the action – transition – transformation model

Another angle for deciding how best to showcase your offer builds on what we discussed earlier about focusing on the transformational benefit you are providing.

Why not make this transformation the nub of the way you craft your customer proposition and USP (unique selling point).

So, if you are a health and fitness coach, don't just focus on the next *'action'* – getting your client to go to the gym.

And don't just talk about achieving the first *'transition'* for your client – losing 10lbs.

Instead, focus on the *'transformation'* you are providing – making them feel more confident in themselves and helping them achieve a range of big life goals.

Unlock the emotional barriers to purchase

Another perspective in helping you sharpen up your messaging – explaining why you are different – is to focus on the emotional barriers that may stand in the way of purchase.

These could include customer anxiety about whether they are making the right decision. Here, you can use approaches like testimonials, references, guarantees and demonstrations to reassure people.

Dial up your differentiating service excellence

Another angle for showcasing your offer is to zero in on the superior way you deliver what it is you do.

The reality is that it is not always possible to have a truly unique selling point: to have a better product than the competition. But if you can't be better – be different.

And one way to do this is to showcase small but powerful service advantages you can provide.

Build a reputation for going the extra mile with personal service extras that make all the difference. Create experiences that mean your customers will want to spread the news to others about why people should buy from you rather than someone else.

Little things make a big difference: A ski shop illustration

A skier on the last day of his ski trip finds a fastening on his ageing ski boots is faulty. Replacement boots of the type he would have bought next are not available in the local ski shop.

But the ski shop owner decides he can do a running repair to allow the skier to enjoy his last day of skiing with his friends. The owner does not cajole the customer into buying replacement boots of a type he doesn't really want.

As soon as the skier gets home he orders online a complete set of ski equipment from this ski shop for the next season. He valued the way the ski shop owner had gone the extra mile to make the last day of his ski trip with his friends possible.

Create a compelling Elevator Pitch

Explaining very succinctly why you are different – why customers should choose you – is critically important.

Here in order to effectively differentiate your offer to customers it is helpful to have an Elevator Pitch.

The Elevator Pitch is the way you would describe your business on a short elevator ride to someone who knows nothing about you or your business.

Many business owners get so caught up in running their business day-to-day that they fail to be totally clear about exactly what it is that differentiates them from their competitors – and how to explain this in a few memorable words.

Preparing an Elevator Pitch will help crystalise the transformational benefit that you will be providing.

The following template will help you.

Your Elevator Pitch template

- We work with…

- They have a problem with…

- What we do is…

- So, that…

- Which means…

- And the reasons they believe in us is…

Illustration: A fitness training business

Below we apply the Elevator Pitch template to a fitness training business.

We work with . . . stressed-out, time-poor senior executives

They have a problem with . . . keeping fit

What we do is . . . design bespoke health and fitness programmes that suit their busy schedules

So that . . . they can get fit and healthy in only 30 minutes a day

Which means . . . they can excel in their careers <u>and</u> also enjoy their family life

The reason they believe in us is . . . we have success testimonials from top executives

By completing just six statements for your business, you can quickly create your own *powerful* Elevator Pitch.

Your Elevator Pitch on a postage stamp

You could then reduce this Elevator Pitch down to one sentence. Staying with our fitness training example:

> *'We fast-track business executives back to fitness and health with bespoke programmes that fit their schedules.'*

Putting in the time to hone to perfection – polish – the exact words you will use to communicate your differentiated offer is critical to your success.

Ensure your website passes the seven-second test

Typically a customer initially only spends seven seconds on a website in deciding whether or not the product or service on offer is for them. This means that – within these few seconds – your website must establish:

○ **Who this website is for**? Can the customer recognise themselves as being in the target audience?

○ **What product/service/benefit is being provided:** Is it instantly clear exactly what you offer – are you a painter of houses or a painter of portraits?

○ **Why should they care?** What is it that is different, special or unique about what you do?

○ **What should they do next?** What is the call to action?

So make sure your website passes the seven-second test.

Some website assessment questions:

The following questions will help you assess how well your website is differentiating your product or service.

Ask: Does your website…

… make you stand out, provide a hook and have a call to action?

… demonstrate that you are really innovative and explain why you are different?

… explain the transformation that your product offers – highlighting the benefits and added value you provide?

… provide visual stimulus as well as just words?

… have the wow factor - come across as truly exciting and aspirational?

… convey your brand values?

… provide the taste and feel of what's special about your product?

… communicate the personal experience you provide?

… demonstrate that you are easy to deal with and have simple and intuitive-to-use products?

… show the value for money you are providing?

… set up a story/narrative that will draw people to you?

… provide social proof – evidence of why your distinctiveness and ability to solve the customer's problem is true.

Put communicating why you are different at the top of the list

In a highly competitive marketplace the elegance, precision and creativity you bring to explaining why you are different is critical.

This is why we have reviewed different ways in which you can showcase your difference. We have looked at ensuring you are eliminating any confused thinking about what you should and should not be saying to your customers.

We highlighted the power of differentiating around the transformation you provide. We looked at reducing any emotional barriers to purchase. And we reviewed the opportunities to dial up the extra service you provide.

And critically we spelt out how to create a compelling differentiating 'Elevator Pitch. We also provided some tips on how to give your website impact. We drove home the importance of ensuring your website does you justice. It must showcase – celebrate – your difference.

Putting energy into showing why you are different will give you a massive competitive advantage.

Key actions

✓ Focus on why you are different by demonstrating the transformational benefits you provide for your customers.

✓ Explain why customers should buy from you in a short Elevator Pitch.

✓ Ensure your website passes the seven-second test.

→ *Stand out from the crowd. Do not shrink from boldly showcasing how your offer is superior to your competitors.*

PART FIVE: BE DIFFERENT
Recap

Add creative edge

We started by looking at the role of creativity in pushing up the chances of making your idea happen. As the world becomes more globalised, standardised and commoditised, your ability to provide a creative edge to your offer will pay massive dividends.

Here a source of inspiration is Julia Cameron, the author of *The Artist's Way*. In her career she has helped many people to start believing in their ability to be creative. She talks about *'creativity being oxygen for our souls'* and about *'finding the river, and saying yes to its flow, rapids and all.'* She is inspiring us to identify those spaces, points in time and moods where we will feel inspired to add that extra spark of creativity to what we are doing.

Touch their world

We looked at the importance of understanding – being in tune with – customers' needs. Here, the late pioneering entrepreneur Anita Roddick, who founded the Body Shop, springs to mind as an inspirational example. Her empathy and genuineness meant she was able to tap into the changing needs of customers in the health & beauty sector and build a successful business empire, whilst remaining true to her values and principles.

Showcase your difference

We concluded by ensuring you showcase your difference. A company that stands out here is Virgin Atlantic. Its theme is 'See the world differently'. Virgin's purpose and values reads: 'We look for unexpected ways to delight. We love connecting with people. We believe thoughtful little touches add up to a big difference'. At every customer touchpoint, Virgin seeks to demonstrate why it is different from more traditional airlines.

PART SIX: BE INFLUENTIAL
Overview

Influence is our inner ability to lift people up to our perspective.
Joseph Wong

16. Be authentic

We start by discussing in more depth the idea of you becoming a 'brand'. Here the brand could be you as a 'personal' brand – the way you identify yourself as a freelancer – or a brand that represents your business. Either way, in your role as a 'brand', you need to start thinking about being an influential presence – and doing this with authenticity.

We recognise that conversations about being influential often raise concerns about whether this is some kind of manipulation: persuading people to do things that they don't necessarily want to do. But influence is not this. It is about constructive thinking on different issues – with integrity and authenticity – in a way that benefits not only you as the entrepreneur, but also others.

17. Tell your story

Here we explain how to tell your brand story in an influential way with impact and genuineness. This is about creating excitement around your own entrepreneurial journey. This will give you a point of difference and help ensure your ideas happen.

So our aim is to give you the confidence to become an influential voice in today's fast moving and complex communications world. You need to be someone who people will listen to, can learn from and respect.

18. Stay relevant

We look at how to keep the story of your emerging brand – the promises you are making to your customers – relevant and in touch with stakeholders' changing needs.

16: BE AUTHENTIC
Highlights

Think of yourself as a brand

You are now a **'brand' offering value** - not someone selling their time for a fee.

You are creating a **valuable asset**.

So get total clarity around what your brand represents. This will be the **golden thread** that runs through your communications.

Build brand authenticity

Your brand is a set of promises that you're making about your product or service. It's a **reflection of your personality** - the way that you will be known and remembered.

What your brand is promising **needs to be true** to who you are as a person – your values and principles.

There needs to be a **synergy** between the business - the brand you are creating – and you the person.

Clear memorable brand messaging

Your brand promise – message – **needs to reflect your personality** in a clear, concise and memorable way.

Keep polishing your brand messaging until you feel it's landing what you want to say.

ENROL A CRITICAL FRIEND: It's difficult at first to think of yourself as a brand – you can be too close. So, invite a friend to critically review how you are presenting your brand – its impact and authenticity.

Be authentic

Authenticity is about being true to who you are, even when everyone around you wants you to be someone else.

Michael Jordan

A big shift in making the transition from employee to being your own boss is the need to start thinking about yourself as a brand.

Some may be planning to set up a 'personal brand' as a way of promoting their products or services – linking your offer to your own name.

Others may have aspirations towards setting up a brand to represent your company. Either way you will need to ensure that your brand is authentic.

In today's highly competitive environment, ensure you carve out a brand that differentiates you from the crowd, but in a way that strikes a powerful authentic chord. There needs to be a synergy between the brand you're creating and who you are as a person.

So, you need to be clear on the values you stand for and make sure that the brand you build offers features and benefits that reflect these values.

Your brand is a promise you make

Your brand is a reflection of you – the platform for being influential

Your brand needs nurturing – it's a valuable asset

Commit to building an authentic brand

When we talk about being a brand, we are not talking about creating a logo. A 'brand' is much bigger than this. Your brand is the way that you will be known and remembered. It's a reflection of your personality.

Your brand is a mixture of both explicit and implicit promises that you're making about the product or service you offer. It is a statement of the way your brand will be recognised at an emotional level.

The brand is at the heart of what many businesses are all about. Therefore the way you create and position your brand needs careful thought.

Questions to help you shape an authentic brand

What does your brand believe in?

What does your brand stand for – what is its stance?

What are the core values that you want reflected in your brand – these will be the golden thread that runs through your business?

What is the inspirational promise that you want your brand to deliver to every stakeholder?

What emotions do you want your brand to evoke in others – what is the overall feeling you want people who use your brand to experience?

What features of your brand that make you different from your competitors do you want to showcase in your branding?

Illustration: Consignia – a brand that lacked authenticity

Consignia was the name selected to be the collective brand to represent the much loved Royal Mail, Post Office, and also Parcelforce, brands.

The name Consignia was conjured up but it was based on *'inside-out thinking'*. It came from people who lived in the world of *'consigning'* parcels and *consignee* notes.

However, if they had looked from the *'outside-in'* customer perspective they would have known that word consign is not generally used in a positive way. It did not relate to the customers' world.

When customers do use the word consign, it is usually in a negative way: a failing football manager is 'consigned to history'.

Ordinary people immediately felt that the decision to use the name Consignia was contrived. It was not genuine and authentic. Consequently Consignia was therefore heavily criticised in the media and later withdrawn and consigned to the rubbish bin.

Ensure your brand is congruent with you

Ensure there is a fundamental synergy between your individual personality and the brand you're promoting.

It's difficult to build a brand that is all about high levels of precision and professionalism if the business owner is rather slapdash and haphazard in their personal approach.

Similarly, creating a brand that is based on being empathetic and listening to the customer will not ring true if the business owner is arrogant and dismissive of others.

One tip is to ask: Is what I, as an *individual,* am going to do next congruent with my *brand* values?

Richard Branson as a personal brand

Richard Branson is a good exemplar when thinking about the relationship between the personality of the business owner and their brand.

In broad terms, the fundamental values of Richard Branson the person – being adventurous, a renegade, and professional – are factors that we can also relate to – and feel comfortable with – when buying the corporate Virgin brand.

Focus your brand on your audience's needs

As we have been stressing, your business – your brand – should focus on the benefits and the transformation you will provide and the outcomes that will result from using your brand rather than someone else's.

Talk about how your brand will benefit the customer. You don't want the presentation of your brand to come across as a glorified *it's all about me* CV – an ego trip where you just focus on your own background and expertise.

Keep your brand 'on point'

One mistake that business owners sometimes make – which we touched on earlier – is to over-communicate with customers and tell them more than they ever wanted to know about their backstory and business operations.

As we highlighted earlier this only leaves the bewildered customer asking themselves *why are they telling me all this?* So if a customer comes into your garden centre to buy a watering can don't overwhelm them with your expertise in underground irrigation systems!

Create a brand message

You can bring clarity to your branding by creating a brand message.

A brand message is a statement that succinctly and memorably captures the values that underpin what it is you do. It is a way of powerfully communicating to your stakeholders and customers your values, standards and what you aspire to.

A fantastic example of a powerful brand message is Mastercard.

> *There are some things money can't buy. For everything else, there's Mastercard.* (The words they crafted here are priceless!)

A framework for developing your brand message

The following framework will help you fashion a brand message.

- ○ **Target audience**: Who are you to talking to – with whom are you trying to communicate?

- ○ **Vision for the brand**: What are you aspiring towards? What are you trying to convey?

- ○ **Brand personality:** What do you want your brand to look and feel like?

- ○ **Brand differentiation:** On which of the factors that are most important to customers does your brand excel?

- ○ **Core brand proposition:** What is the transformational value that your brand is providing?

- ○ **The desired outcome:** What change in your customers' thinking and behaviour do you want your brand to bring about?

Polishing your brand message

To help you craft your brand message to give it the *wow factor*, ask the following questions:

> Does your message genuinely showcase what it is that makes you stand out in the marketplace?

> Is your brand message truly exciting, aspirational and innovative? Is it likely to prompt and encourage people to want to buy from you?

> Does your brand message convey exactly what it would be like to taste and feel what is special about your product or service?

> Does it call out and showcase what is particularly important in your brand offer? (This could be your personal expertise, your brand's simplicity of use, or the value for money you offer.)

> Does your brand message create a buzz?

> Does it have a hook that will make your message stick?

In sum ask: does your brand message get everything over with maximum clarity, the minimum of words with a high level of memorability?

Let's look at two illustrations of the importance of getting over a message that is simple, in the customer's own language and is likely to 'stick'.

Illustration: A bookshop brand message

Let's look at creating a brand message for a children's bookshop in a small town.

One option is to go with a solid but fairly bland, ordinary and earnest statement along the following lines:

- *We are an established family-run business that has been trading since 1972 and have a wide range of reasonably price children's books and we enjoy talking to customers about which books are best for their children.*

But look at how much more impactful the brand message could be after some crisp thinking and creativity.

- *We make reading fun - if kids enjoy books, they will want to read more.*

Illustration: A gentleman's tailor brand message

And now let's look at an example of creating a brand message for an exclusive gentleman's tailor.

One approach could be to explain the intricacies of your own process:

- *We are professional tailors who use the latest profile stitching machines and premium wool blended fabrics.*

Talking about the intricacies of tailoring is all very worthy but it is a bit introspective and boring.

In contrast an improved version which focuses on getting 'lean-in' from the customer could be:

- *Whether you are one of our top celebrity clients or buying your first ever suit, you'll feel a million dollars wearing one of our world-class suits.*

The lesson here is to work hard to make your key brand message stand out. So take your initial message and polish it until it shines. You need to be on top of how to create crisp and punchy communications that will stick in the memory. You will not regret investing time in word crafting.

Deliver your brand promises – consistently walk the talk

Always deliver the fundamental promises that underpin your brand message. In this way you build authenticity and trust.

Let's take the example of a health clinic that positions itself by saying:

We offer the best patient care to every patient every time.

This is a fantastic brand message because it is punchy, whilst spelling out concrete performance criteria on which the clinic can be judged and on which it must deliver. The clinic is committing to what it must provide for its patients and knows it must consistently live up to these promises.

Be consistent in your messaging

Building on the theme of delivering your brand promises, there needs to be consistency in the way your brand message is presented. Inconsistencies in the way your brand is represented across different channels and scenarios will build doubt and lower trust.

The customer will want to see the same brand values being conveyed – represented – in the brand communications you have on your shop front, your website and on any delivery vehicles you may have and so on.

Take entrepreneurial ownership for managing your brand

Creating a brand message is the start of your brand journey. But you then need to manage the way your brand will evolve and be perceived over time in the marketplace.

So make sure you get regular customer feedback. This will ensure that a gap does not gradually build between what you think your brand represents and what customers actually experience about your brand on the ground.

Here it's helpful to enrol a critical friend to walk through your brand experience and provide you with regular feedback about where you need to make enhancements to square up your brand promises with your actual delivery in the marketplace.

The world welcomes authenticity

Today, in building a personal brand or company brand, you need to make an impact but, more than ever, you also need to demonstrate genuineness and authenticity.

We live in a world where businesses are expected to be sensitive to environmental, social and cultural issues and seen to be good citizens.

In addition, these days increasingly businesses are expected to demonstrate what it is they believe in rather than sitting on the fence and being neutral.

Successful entrepreneurship requires you to be clear on what you stand for – and for you to be courageous in defending your principles.

Be authentic and true to your values at all times and act with integrity.

But fine judgements are called for in deciding whether or not to get involved with controversial issues about which you feel passionate, but that could impact negatively on your brand and business. Here think 'Choice Moment' and maybe talk any dilemmas through with a 'critical friend' before making your final decision.

Key actions

✓ Get total clarity around what your brand represents – it's values. This is at the heart of what your business is all about.

✓ Recognise that your brand is a promise you are making to customers. This needs to be authentic and reflect your personality.

✓ Look after your brand – cultivate and cherish it. It could end up as a very valuable asset for you.

→ *Start thinking about yourself as a brand and the relationship between you – the person – and you the brand.*

17: TELL YOUR STORY
Highlights

Marketing is your business

The ability to do a good professional job is a necessary, but not sufficient, condition of success. **You've got to be in the marketing game.**

Marketing, selling and promoting your business is, in a way, **more important than the core product or service** you are offering.

You need to showcase - shout about - why it is customers should choose you over your competitors. You need to **dial up your strengths -** accentuate the positives. If you don't, you won't have a business or any customers!

Share your story

Today **compelling stories** are the way stakeholders and customers want to hear about products and services.

Your own **entrepreneurial journey** is a story you should tell.

Mastering the craft of storytelling will provide you with a competitive advantage.

Put yourself into the story

Emotion plays a big part in people's decision with whom to do business. So don't be afraid to put some of yourself into the story you're telling about your brand.

Be clear how you come across in different marketing and social media channels. Ensure that everything you say and do **supports your vision, values and goals.**

You need to be **liked and respected** as someone people will want to do business with - you can enjoy selling without being too salesy.

THE FUTURE BELONGS TO STORYTELLERS: Stories are the way we make sense of the world

Tell your story

A person can have the greatest idea in the world – completely different and novel – but if that person can't convince enough other people, it doesn't matter.

Gregory Berns

Continuing with the theme of this part of the book – being influential – we now look at the power of being able to tell the story of your brand in an impactful way.

This starts by accepting that success on your entrepreneurial journey will hinge on your ability to influence and persuade with authenticity.

History is littered with examples of talented individuals with great ideas – masters of their craft – who failed to get over their message because they were not fluent communicators. They had great insights, but they could not influence and persuade others to their point of view.

Recognise that being influential and persuasive – telling your story – is an entirely legitimate undertaking. It is not one from which you should shrink.

Do not have any reservations about promoting your point of view – influencing others

Tap into your customer's emotions

Tell your brand's story in a compelling way

Prioritise the marketing and promotion of your business

Many small businesses get caught up in the detail of what it is they do rather than prioritise the marketing and promotion of their business. It is difficult for them to accept that *marketing* what they do is, in a way, more important than *doing* what they do.

There is a need to recognise that those with the most powerful insights and ideas do not necessarily receive the greatest reward. The reward often goes to those who are best able to communicate an idea and influence others.

So it is worth investing time in becoming a really effective communicator. Do not be the person who has fantastic ideas but who cannot make these happen because they resist acquiring the skills needed to be a fluent communicator.

Here, take comfort in the fact that one of the world's greatest presenters, Steve Jobs, admitted that he wasn't a natural presenter. He worked at it because he knew being influential and persuasive was so vitally important to his success.

The Semmelweis story

Dr Ignaz Semmelweis, in 1847, was the first to identify that disease could be transferred contagiously, not just through the air. He recognised that if doctors washed their hands between operations this would reduce death rates.

But he was not a natural communicator, and it was Pasteur some years later, who was better able to communicate this idea, who ended up getting most of the credit.

This may seem very unfair, but the reality is that you need to buy into the power of being influential and persuasive in order to get your ideas off the ground.

Communicate with powerful business stories

Over the last decade or so business has been won over by the power of storytelling. Seth Godin says, *'Marketing is no longer about the stuff you make, but about the stories that you tell.'*

Being an influencer and having the ability to create powerful communications requires you to structure elegant storylines.

Stories are powerful because they:

○ **Make messages stick:** They engage with stakeholders' emotions, get 'lean-in' and make it easier for the audience to grasp and remember the key message – headline – you are landing.

○ **Inspire action:** Stories uplift and motivate audiences which means stakeholders are more likely to take action on your message.

○ **Encourage the sharing of your message:** Entertaining stories that strike a chord are more likely to be shared with others – people enjoy relaying and being associated with powerful motivational stories.

Stories are the way we make sense of the world

○ We don't remember too much about the Greeks, but we do remember the story of the Trojan Horse.

○ We don't recall the details of Newton's theory of gravity, but we do remember the story of Isaac Newton and the apple.

○ We don't remember the twists and turns of the USA vs USSR space race, but we do remember the story of Neil Armstrong's first step on the moon.

In sum, stories work – they are a powerful communication tool.

Acquire the art of crafting a compelling story

Taking time out to develop the skill of telling engaging stories in a business context will pay dividends. This is a big topic but below we briefly touch on a couple of key principles.

Clarity over the purpose of your communication

The start point for creating a compelling business story that will engage your audience is to be clear on the fundamental purpose of the communication.

Here, when we are using the word 'purpose', we are referring to what overall change it is you want to bring about in your audience by delivering this communication. Having this *'definiteness of purpose'* is the foundation of all successful communications.

To make this point concrete let us take an illustration. So let us say you are a consultant addressing a business challenge set by a client. Then clearly you have the immediate communications goal of providing a solution to this challenge – let's say explaining that Option A is a better solution than Option B.

But your overarching *purpose* in this example is to be seen as the person who has lowered your client's anxiety and stress levels and helped him make and action the right decision. This is the ultimate *'purpose'* of your communication. Your story should be working to achieve this.

Become familiar with story structures to drive your communications

There is an architecture to an elegant story. Stories follow a structure – one that takes the audience on a journey (as in a film or play). You need to understand the craft of structuring a compelling story.

Your audience will warm to a storyline that sets out the context, outlines the choices that need to addressed and leads the audience through to a solution, whilst at different points in your story, creating *lean-in* moments where you strike a powerful emotional chord.

People switch off when there is a disjointed account of events. What the audience wants is a flowing natural narrative that arcs through to a concluding call to action.

I Have a Dream

One example of the power of structure in telling your story is in Martin Luther King's *I Have a Dream* speech. This speech has a compelling rhythmic *architecture.*

First, he sets up a *challenge (problem)* – the black community in the US are being treated unfairly. Then he moves on to discuss *a solution* – the arrival of the Civil Rights movement campaigning for equality. He then has a *call to action.*

And everything is brilliantly tied together with his compelling repetition throughout of his *I have a dream* theme.

Add a twist with your storytelling

Earlier with our gentleman's tailors example we dialled up the importance in telling your story with brevity. Ditch the detail and cut to the chase: 'Our suits make you feel like a million dollars.'

But let us now turn this on its head and provide an illustration of how to use technical detail to tell a story with a hook to land a message that will stick.

Illustration: Brighton Beau Shirts

Brighton Beau produce top end of the range high-quality shirts that are sold for a premium price.

Here is the story the company came up with to hit home what goes into making a quality shirt and in so doing 'justify' their premium pricing strategy:

WHY NOT MAKE YOUR OWN BRIGHTON BEAU SHIRT - IT'S SIMPLE: HERE'S HOW TO DO IT...

We know our world-class high-quality shirts are premium priced so we thought you might want to make one for yourself and save yourself some money... so here is what you need to do...

- Travel to Italy to source the most luxurious selection of quality fabrics and then have them woven to our own unique specification using our leading-edge shirt design software created for us by specialists in San Francisco.

- Purchase a state-of-the-art Pollino 2800 precision cutting machine from Switzerland. It is the best but unfortunately the most expensive: £100,000 should cover it – but don't forget it's a Brighton Beau shirt you are after.

- To stitch together the 37 individual pieces that go into a Brighton Beau shirt we recommend the Adler 956 deluxe sewing machine for the pockets and a Durkopp 862 for your collars. And for those tricky buttonholes you can't beat the Rimoldi 294. And to tackle the intricate French seams, our master shirtmakers swear by the Necci BEX. It's complicated to use but does a brilliant job and is what makes a Brighton Beau a shirt to die for!

So you are now good to get started: we reckon that after six months or so practice with this superb machinery and hot-off-the-press software you will eventually get the hang of it. BUT if don't want to wait this long and shell out so much money on software and machinery, we have an idea:

WHY NOT JUST VISIT YOUR LOCAL STOCKIST AND PURCHASE A BRIGHTON BEAU FROM US!

It is instantly available at a fraction of the cost.

Here at Brighton Beau on the South Coast of England, with our expert craftsmen, experience and equipment, we have been fashioning the finest Brighton Beau shirts since 1898.

You get the idea!

Engaging storytelling is a fantastic way to stand out from the crowd, get lean-in and drive home your brand story!

Embrace showtime

After structuring a compelling storyline you now need to tell your story in an engaging way. You need to acquire the ability to be present in the moment: be there for your audience. You need to know how to switch into *'showtime':* give your audience your total presence.

Getting into showtime – being 'present' – could be on a video call or at a face-to-face business presentation. But whatever the gig it's important to show up with energy, self-belief and confidence.

You need to know how to turn up with your A-Game when it counts. Remember, your audience can always smell desperation. So you need to polish your performance so it effortlessly flows and know how to deliver it in a memorable way. Take time out to cultivate these skills. They are a key part of being a successful entrepreneur.

Connect, uplift, praise

When you are in front of an audience focus on making sure that you demonstrate presence, connect with people, uplift everyone's spirits and praise the individuals around you for their efforts.

Be there in the moment

In winning over and engaging an audience cultivate the habit of giving individuals, customers, stakeholders and colleagues your total concentration.

Don't be only *half* concentrating on them. Audiences can sense whether you're clearly listening, focusing and responding to them, as opposed to half concentrating on something else. As they say, *be here now. Be someplace else later!*

A lesson: Elvis's walk

Why not take a leaf out of Elvis's book. When on tour, in order to put himself into '*showtime*' mode he would have his Winnebago (mobile dressing room trailer) parked one thousand yards from the performance stage. It was during the '*1000 yard walk*' from his trailer to the stage that Elvis got focused and left the trials and tribulations of day-to-day life behind him. He thought himself into '*showtime*' mode and became 'Elvis'.

Operate with a social media strategy

Today's social media culture provides you with wonderful opportunities to communicate your brand's story in a range of different formats including Facebook, Instagram, Twitter, LinkedIn and WhatsApp.

But this shouldn't be a random haphazard set of posts. Everything needs to be organised. There should be a golden thread of clear, well-thought-out messaging running through your communications.

On the one hand you need to stay creative and a little edgy: provide fresh ideas and show how you're different. But on the other hand this needs to be done in an informed and controlled way.

Don't fall victim to an off the cuff ill-thought-through emotional outburst – rant – that could lead to a negative backlash.

Manage social media fans, strangers and haters

You can please some of the people some of the time, but not all of the people all of the time. So, you need to get your head around how to make social media work for you.

In summary, your social media activity will probably attract three kinds of response:

Fans: people who know you and like your brand and what you are doing. This is of course good news, but here make sure that you do not *only* listen to feedback from this group and believe everything they say. You need to take this praise with a pinch of salt.

Strangers: People who do not know you but who are important because they could be a major potential customer. Here you need to understand where they are coming from. Their feedback could be particularly helpful because it could be more objective than feedback coming from your 'fans' and provide clues about how you could improve.

Haters: However good, reasonable, authentic and genuine your product or service is, there will be individuals who decide (for whatever weird reasons) to leave destructive and hurtful comments. Haters are an unfortunate biproduct of the arrival of social media.

Moreover, these dysfunctional individuals often acquire a following whereby a negative 'herd' mentality kicks in. So, as an entrepreneur, you need to develop the mental resilience to cope with negativity.

So in sum, don't restrict yourself to just acting on what your 'fans' say. Learn from constructive criticism from 'strangers'. But don't get demoralised by what the 'haters' and their followers say.

And most importantly, don't fall into the trap of responding with an overly emotional ill-thought-out retort.

Be an influential authority in your field

Cultivating a thought leadership persona will pay dividends and help you build your brand. By thought leadership, we're not necessarily talking about coming up with ground-breaking new theories or devastatingly new solutions.

We're talking about demonstrating to your customers and key stakeholders that you are constantly engaging with, and thinking about, the big trends and issues that are facing your market.

Assuming this leadership, rather than follower, role in your sector will generate customer confidence. Customers will turn to you as the authority for solutions rather than to others.

Your reflections and observations about events and developments will help indicate to customers that you are a person they can trust and look to for a solution to their own specific problems.

So, if you are in the business of fitting solar panels, start writing blogs and posts that indicate you are aware of the overall trends taking place in this marketplace.

Then begin to translate this knowledge into a few little tips and tricks – hints, clues and ideas – that you share on your website in order to demonstrate to customers that you are the person with whom they should be doing business.

The problem… solution… problem… technique

One technique to consider in building your authority is the *'problem and solutions'* technique. Here you set out a problem that you solve (for free) and then do this again (again for free). Then set up a problem that you leave hanging (and do not solve for free).

The idea here is that because of the credibility you have built up in solving earlier problems, this could lead your customer to talk to you – rather than your competitors – about tackling this outstanding problem (whilst also being prepared to pay you!)

Tapping into the power of authentic storytelling will help build your authority

Businesses now realise that the best way to engage and make an impact is to tap into the power of storytelling.

The last decade or so has seen a massive shift in the way businesses communicate with their different audiences. Everybody now recognises that the story format is the way many people make sense of the world.

Here our message is that it is important to tell your story with integrity and authenticity.

Your audience will sense whether your story is contrived and made up rather than being an elegant and genuine way of explaining your entrepreneurial journey and what you stand for and represent.

Key actions

- Tap into the power of business storytelling. In a straight choice between emotion and reason, emotion usually wins.

- Do not shrink from being influential and persuasive. Develop the confidence to be a thought leader to whom customers can turn to for reassurance and ideas.

- Always turn up as the best possible version of yourself. Bring your A-Game to everything you do. Put in the time to cultivate these influencing and communication skills.

> *Be here now. Be someplace else later.*
> *How difficult can that be!*

18: STAY RELEVANT
Highlights

Be comfortable with uncertainty

The Entrepreneur Mindset embraces feeling comfortable with uncertainty. Keep up your antennae. It's about anticipating events. **'Chance favours the prepared mind'.**

As an entrepreneur, you must **take personal responsibility** for managing your brand through change - over time.

It's about constantly **sharpening the saw**, engaging in competitive renewal and keeping your brand fresh.

Look out for the accelerating present

It's important to find the time to keep up with how **changing market conditions** may affect your brand.

Being ready for the future is not about being a visionary with a crystal ball. It's about identifying trends that are surfacing - and are likely to accelerate. Then **think through the future implications** of these for your own business.

Always be expecting change - assume that there will be further challenges down the road. Be mentally prepared. **Forewarned is forearmed.**

Ask 'what if' questions

Make sure that you are **prepared for likely future scenarios.**

The **'what if' technique** is powerful - ask what if questions about your business, customers and suppliers.

For example, what would you do if your main supplier can no longer provide you with a critical component? **Always have a Plan B.**

FORECASTING HAS ITS CRITICS: 'He who lives by the crystal ball soon learns to eat ground glass!' (But you do need to think ahead!)

Stay relevant

*It is not the strongest of the species that survives,
not the most intelligent that survives.
It is the one that is the most adaptable to change.*

Charles Darwin

Building your reputation as an influential entrepreneur includes being comfortable with change and keeping your brand relevant.

You need to keep your antennae up to look for signals that are telling you that you need to adapt and pivot your brand in order to evolve with the changing environment.

Here we're not talking about being a mystic with a crystal ball who can see the future but cultivating a mindset that effortlessly embraces uncertainty. Successful entrepreneurs enjoy anticipating change and in this way they are poised to seize opportunities in a timely way. Pasteur said, '*Chance favours the prepared mind.'*

Accept and be prepared for constant change

Keep scanning the horizon to pinpoint 'plausible possible futures' and opportunities

Follow up your monitoring of changing events with action

Be comfortable with being uncomfortable

Cultivating a robust mindset that is comfortable with change is critical. Think of this as being 'comfortable with being uncomfortable'. It is about always being prepared to pivot in order to respond to changing circumstances.

Accepting that change and disruption is a fact of business life and recognising that you must keep your brand fresh is a key component of the Entrepreneur Mindset.

You need to be constantly *sharpening the saw* and engaging in competitive renewal. It's about anticipating what might go wrong and being ready to deal with events.

'Events' are always just around the corner. As is said of history, '*It's just one damn thing after another!*' So it's about accepting that just when things are in place, things could change yet again. It's about <u>not</u> expecting everything to go according to plan and factoring this into the way you prepare for each day.

Keep your antennae up and learn to read the signals

Keep on your radar what's happening in your marketplace. Take time out to look at wider global macro trends. See how these may trickle down to affect your own business.

Isaiah Berlin refers to visionary leaders – entrepreneurs – as having '*An acute sense of what fits with what, what springs from what, and what leads to what.*'

The aim is to futureproof your brand. But by this we do *not* mean keeping the future out – like waterproofing. We are instead entreating you to embrace the future – understand the prevailing winds of change and always be prepared to adapt and pivot. Wayne Gretzky, the ice hockey superstar, said, '*I skate to where the puck is going to be, not to where it has just been.*'

Check out experts and commentators on your market: read the editorials in trade magazines. See what various consumer watchdog organisations are saying. Attend industry events run by trade associations and network at conferences and seminars.

Ask yourself questions about national, market and local trends

> **National level trends**: What is happening to overall customer spending levels – what, if any, are the implications for my industry?

> **Market and sector trends:** What is happening in my supply chain and what are the implications for me?

> **Local conditions:** What is the biggest threat and opportunity here (e.g. Is the Local Council likely to change my business rates?)

Keep your head above the parapet

Many business owners get caught up in the *weeds*. They will be working IN their business and not find the time to get their head above the parapet and work ON their business. They will bury their head in the sand and fail to keep an eye on bigger trends and think through the implications for their business.

Let's take the example of a small garage servicing petrol and diesel cars where the order book is pretty full for the next month or so. Here it's easy to ignore the implications of when we arrive at the tipping point when the majority of cars will be electric. Do you have plans in place to deal with this transition?

And for many of us – from advertising copywriters to lawyers – there is now the challenge of learning how to work alongside generative AI, such as ChatGPT.

Ask 'what if' questions about critical dimensions of your product/service

A powerful technique for staying relevant is to ask a series of *what if* questions about your market, customers, suppliers and processes. Then make sure you're prepared for what might occur in the future.

For example, you could ask what you would do if your main supplier was unable to provide you with what you need. What is your plan B?

Another illustration might be asking how you will respond if the industry standard for the speed of supplying a particular service in your sector was halved in the next year? And if an automated AI version of your core skillset suddenly became available. What would your response be?

171

Learn from your competitors and customers

Monitoring your competition is another lens through which to read and anticipate change. Identify which players in the marketplace are making the biggest changes and establish why are they doing this? Pinpoint what is the biggest thing that is happening in your competitive space and think through what it is you should now be doing about it.

Look at how your customers are coping with changing customer priorities and ask what is the number one difference between consumers now, and what you sense consumers will want next year? Does this have any implications for the way you organise your own internal processes and ways of working?

And why not identify a leading-edge competitor that you admire and that you yourself like doing business with and study them closely. What is it that they excel at in meeting customers' needs and requirements? See whether this sparks ideas on how you can develop and futureproof your own brand.

For example, this may reveal that you are still relying on conventional e-mail to promote your products/services. Whereas the leading competitors are now sending high impact BombBomb videos to showcase their wares.

Identify the opportunities in disruption

As a business owner you need to be on the lookout for disruptor strategies: the sudden arrival of a totally new way of thinking about solving a problem and/or offering a service that transforms current business models.

For example, Uber suddenly disrupted the life of London cab drivers by changing the paradigm. This was more than now being able to call up the taxi/car on an app. The arrival of Uber meant that you could now also track the progress of the taxi making its way to you. Uber now provided *certainty*. It made the idea of standing in the street in the hope of waving down a taxi less attractive.

So be alert to underlying market and customer trends – disruption – that could transform your business model. But remember that although disruptors can be a threat they could also open up new opportunities.

172

So begin to identify something that, if it happened over the next few months, would dramatically affect your business for the worse. Then start by reviewing any *obstacles* that this would create for you. But then begin to focus on the *opportunities* that this disruption could open up for you.

'There is a tide in the affairs of men, which taken at the flood, leads on to fortune.'
William Shakespeare

Illustration: Finding opportunities in disruption - A hotel's response to Airbnb

Airbnb is a classic disrupter example. By opening up the range of accommodation people can now access when travelling on holiday or business it forced hotels to rethink their business model - seek out new opportunities.

For instance, a small hotel, to counter Airbnb, has the opportunity to provide comprehensive value for money room service throughout the day. This will appeal to putative Airbnb customers who do not want to get involved in cooking and food preparation.

A small hotel could also focus on the fact that they have *lots of communal space* and facilities available for different group activities - this might not be the case in someone's home.

The hotel could also focus on the *guaranteed security* provided by being an established hotel, taking away the worry about whether the Airbnb option is in a safe area.

More radically, the hotel could *convert some of their hotel rooms into short term rentals*, possibly adding a kitchen facility. You get the idea. Disruption opens up opportunities.

So the trick is to not think of disruption as an insurmountable obstacle. Instead view it through the lens of what *opportunities* this could open up for you.

Look out for the accelerating present

Keep a close eye on how leading-edge technology – such as Artificial Intelligence and augmented reality – is beginning to impact on your sector.

Think of your task as picking up clues about the 'accelerating present'. This is about learning from those already experimenting with the latest technology and then working through the likely future implications for your own business.

Study those who are in the vanguard of driving forward your own industry or sector: pick up 'insights' about what these early adopters and front runners are doing. Then think through what this means for your own business moving forward.

To illustrate what we mean by studying the 'accelerating present' let's take the example of a marketing agency specialising in advising customers on how best to showcase the customer experience.

Here, we can expect a massive increase in the use of augmented reality. Customers can now live and feel the brand experience in the virtual world. So if you are a marketing agency in this field, why not start checking out the leading augmented reality players, learn from them and apply this to your own business.

Examples of <u>not</u> reading the accelerating present

Kodak was in a fantastic position to make the transition from traditional photography into the digital image-making era. But it failed to read the rate of change and do the right things at the right time.

Similarly Blockbuster was in a great position to make the transition from people renting videos into the world of streaming. But they didn't act in a timely way, thereby allowing Netflix and Amazon to lead the way.

The future was staring Kodak and Blockbuster in the face but they both failed to read the signals and pivot.

Ensure you stay fresh and energised

The entrepreneurial journey can be a roller coaster ride. You start with the excitement of thinking big and being visionary about your hopes and dreams for your business. But you can then get dragged down into the weeds where each day becomes about firefighting and paying the bills on time.

So, to offset this slide into blinkered short-term thinking, reflect on how you will sustain your own energy and enthusiasm levels. What will you do to keep your head above the parapet and focused on the changing horizons. This is all part and parcel of keeping your business relevant.

Some ideas here include keeping yourself energised by taking time out to listen to motivational speakers who will re-vitalise you and keep you fresh. It is about spending time with high energy 'make it happen' people, rather than energy robbers who bring you down.

So why not pick an inspirational event, put it in your calendar and, even though you have a lot of day-to-day pressures, make sure you always find time to turn up.

Living with uncertainty

Having successfully got your entrepreneurial venture off the ground it is alas wishful thinking to believe that from thereon out everything will remain stable and set. The reality is that security is an illusion. Uncertainty is today's reality. The ability to constantly deal with disruption and change is a hallmark of the successful entrepreneur.

So having a mindset that is comfortable with being uncomfortable – accepting change – is a key part of the entrepreneur's make up. It is about constantly scanning the horizon to anticipate change so that you continue to stay relevant as your entrepreneurial venture evolves.

Entrepreneurial life is much like politics, there are always going to be 'events' happening each day and week to which you need to respond.

As an entrepreneur, you need to be stoic. A British Prime Minister described his role as Premier as akin to taking part in a child's game where you have to *simultaneously* get three silver balls into three holes in a dish. Just as you get the last silver ball in place, the first one you put in pops out!

The lesson here is that, as an entrepreneur, you can't spend your time craving the moment where everything is in place. In business life – like politics – expect events to come knocking on your door. We live in a world where something is always going to need fixing.

175

Key actions

✓ Take time out to ask critical questions about the implications of trends that could affect your business.

✓ Cultivate the mindset where challenges, problems and disruption are immediately 'processed' as possible opportunities. Remember, uncertainty plus confidence equals creativity.

✓ It's important to look after yourself on your entrepreneurial journey. Make sure you keep the journey enjoyable and inspirational by treating yourself to some big-ticket motivational treats from time to time.

> → *If you don't think about the future – you won't have one!*

PART SIX: BE INFLUENTIAL
Recap

Be authentic

In this part of the book, we focused on being influential. We opened by looking at what it means to build a personal brand that reflects what you stand for and represent – a brand that is totally authentic. Here, if you check out the Patagonia Company you will find a company that from its inception through to its recent sale, illustrates how authenticity has been at the heart of the brand's success.

Tell the story

Next we highlighted the power of storytelling in becoming an influential brand. Storytelling lies at the heart of many successful marketing communications.

To reinforce this point we highlighted the way Lego recognised that grandparents, parents and children all shared stories about how they grew up playing with Lego and used the concept of *'play'* as its core story – USP.

Stay relevant

We then looked at how to move with the times and keep your brand relevant. Here McDonald's is an exemplar. It never thought of itself as just being in the business of selling hamburgers. It always realised that it was in the business of acquiring prime property locations and being world leaders in how to scale the distribution of fast food. This means it can constantly change the actual product offer over time, such that the McDonald's menu now offers a range of healthy eating options, including vegan.

PART SEVEN: DELIVER HIGH PERFORMANCE OVERVIEW

Human excellence is a state of mind.

Socrates

19. Make informed decisions

In this last part of the book, we focus on high performance. By high performance we mean 'consistently – over the long term – exceeding standard expectations and results'.

In the opening chapter, we put the spotlight on high performance decision-making. The need for clear deep thinking underpins everything you do as an entrepreneur and here we focus on the art of decision-making: how best to decide between different options.

This act of deciding should not be made in a hasty way but carefully thought through. One tip is to set up 'decision moments' where you allocate a specific date, time and location for framing your decision choices and working through to the optimum decision.

20. Master winning ways

We look in this chapter at how entrepreneurs develop the 'winner's advantage' and avoid the 'loser's curse'. It is about acquiring the skills and knowledge that push up the chances of things going your way. Benjamin Franklin said *'Diligence is the mother of good luck.'*

21. Cultivate success habits

In this last chapter, we discuss how to create success habits on which you can automatically fall back on – almost without thinking – to deal with specific situations. We suggest setting up *'triggers'* to prompt you into playing out the behaviours that make up a key habit.

We aim to inspire you to reach your full potential and realise all the possibilities open to you.

19: MAKE INFORMED DECISIONS
Highlights

Enjoy thinking and decision-making!

Apply **clear deep accurate thinking** to everything you do.

Don't make decisions on autopilot. It's easy to get preoccupied with day-to-day events and put thinking on the back burner but it is important that **everything is thought through**.

Distinguish between **accurate evidence-based thinking** and sloppy overly emotional thinking that leads to poor knee-jerk decisions.

Go for informed intuition

Some entrepreneurs believe that **intuitive thinking** – gut feel - is superior to rational thinking.

Intuition plays a major role, but some intuitive thinking can just be plain wrong! It can become an excuse for sloppy thinking - so **get the balance right**.

It's helpful to cultivate the idea of **informed intuition**. This is about combining hard facts with flair, creativity and intuition in arriving at a final decision.

Create decision moments

Carve out time and space for clear deep thinking. Smart thinking is a critical part of the entrepreneur's job. Enjoy **thinking for yourself**.

So, **schedule a date and time** in the calendar - and a location - to reflect on and make key decisions.

You can't do this for every micro decision, but you should do this for each **major decision** about your business.

FIND TIME TO THINK: Be willing to put in the thinking time it takes to make your decisions the right ones

Make informed decisions

Decision-making is easy once someone has framed the choices for me.

Lou Gerstner, former IBM Chairman

Some entrepreneurs think that gut feeling and intuition are superior to more logical, rational thinking when it comes to making great decisions. And there are numerous examples of the power of intuitive, creative decision-making.

However, much intuitive thinking can just be plain wrong. It is just simply an excuse for sloppy thinking. Here you could even think of 'gut' thinking as standing for G*iven Up Thinking.*

So the key is to draw on your flair and intuition but to integrate this with clear, deep, accurate thinking. It's about finding that sweet spot between reason and emotion.

You could think of this as *informed intuition.* It's about clear thinking about the hard facts and then allowing flair, creativity and intuition to be factored into the final decision.

Allocate time in your diary for accurate thinking

Combine your evaluation of the facts with your own creative, intuitive flair to arrive at an informed decision

Do your homework on the cognitive influences (biases) we know affect how people think, decide and act

Schedule a date, time and space for accurate thinking

When it comes to decision-making, it is easy to get so preoccupied with day-to-day events that insufficient time and space is allocated for the *act* of making an informed decision.

What happens is that decisions get made *on the run* – in the corridor – while you are rushing to a meeting. Decisions become little more than a hasty knee-jerk emotional reaction.

They are taken without enough elapsed time to reflect on what is actually happening. The result is poor judgement and decision-making that can damage your business.

Create decision moments

Carve out the time and space needed for clear deep thinking prior to decision-making. Here it's good practice to identify a decision that needs to be made and specify a dedicated date and time in the calendar – together with a location – for when you will examine and make this important decision.

You can't do this for every micro decision. But you should do it for major strategic decisions that have long-term consequences for your business.

Ensure you identify and define the true problem

In making sound decisions it is critical to start the process by making sure you're working on the right problem – and not just on the symptoms. If you think the problem is your product, but the true problem is your customer service, then no amount of product improvement is going to solve your problem.

So accurately defining the *true* problem rather than working on the *presented* problem is critical. Albert Einstein is reported as saying, *'If I had an hour to solve a problem, I would spend 55 minutes thinking about the problem and 5 minutes thinking about the solution.'*

So let's look at some different techniques and perspectives to help you interrogate the initially presented problem so you get the heart of what is really going on.

Your role is to crystallise and refine the problem in a way that will make it easier for you to come up with an effective solution.

Definitions and distinctions

A start point to defining the true problem is to precisely *define* your terms. So if the presented problem is 'falling repeat business' then *exactly* how do we define this?

Drawing *distinctions* is another helpful way of adding clarity to the problem definition process. For example it could be helpful to pinpoint what is the exact difference – distinction – between a price *'discount'* (for buying more than a certain amount or for long-term customer loyalty) and a price *'reduction'* (lowering your price for a period of time).

The 'What is the problem I'm solving for?' technique

The following framework will help you reflect on the *presented* problem and help you work towards identifying the *true* problem you're solving for.

What is the problem I'm trying to solve?

Why is this a problem?

What has to be present for the problem to occur?

Have I looked for when and where this problem occurs? And when and where this problem is <u>not</u> present?

What are the consequences of <u>not</u> solving this problem?

What have I tried so far to solve this problem?

What are the lessons here?

How would I know that this was no longer a problem?

What will things look like once this problem has been solved?

Understanding the 'core phenomenon'

Another technique to better understand the true problem is to reflect on the core phenomenon – the principle or big idea – that is underpinning the issue you are exploring.

Here we have already given the illustration of Lego. Once it had identified that *play* was the core phenomenon underpinning its success, it was able to leverage this insight in re-energising the brand.

Unearthing underlying assumptions

Another approach is to work through all of the underlying assumptions that have been made in arriving at the initial statement of the problem.

Ask yourself whether – in the way this problem has been initially presented – an assumption has been made that cannot be validated and therefore needs challenging.

For example, a city centre seeking to attract more visitors may present its 'problem' – barrier to growth – as being insufficient parking spaces in the city centre. But here you need to challenge this assumption. In fact, there could be a variety of other reasons that explain low visitor footfall in the city centre, such as a lack of good value places to eat.

Challenge cherished beliefs

In defining and refining a problem it can be helpful to explore what's behind the fundamental belief structures of the people involved in this issue.

One technique is to first clarify, and make concrete, a belief that is believed to be true. For example, if someone says 'working long hours always leads to success' then ask the following series of questions:

- *Question one:* Why do you believe this to be true? (Then ask this 'Why' question again about the answer provided – and maybe repeat this sequence twice more.)

- *Question two:* Do you always believe this to be true? Or is this only true some of the time?

○ *Question three*: What would need to be true for you to change your belief about this?

Identify information that will improve your decision-making

Robust contextual information is often a route to better decision-making. David Ogilvy, the advertising legend, used to refer to the power of 'data-rich thinking'.

And when it comes to identifying data and information to support quality thinking and decision-making let's recognise that the following – initially baffling – statement by Donald Rumsfeld, former United States Secretary of Defence, is in fact very helpful.

○ There are *known knowns*: things we know that we know.

○ There are *known unknowns*: things that we know we don't know.

○ But there are also *unknown unknowns*: things we don't know that we don't know.

Start by identifying *what it is you know* – the 'known knowns'. It is sensible not to reinvent the wheel: so check out what easily available information will help you with your decision.

Next think about *what is unknown,* but if it was known, would be helpful to you in making this decision – the 'known unknowns'.

Thinking in this way will help you prioritise the information gaps. What are the big ticket things we would like to know but currently don't know? How much better will our decision be if we obtained this information?

You can now make decisions about whether it is practicable, economical and a good return on investment to start acquiring this priority information.

The next part of the process is to acknowledge that critical uncertainties could be heading your way. Here, as mentioned earlier, you could check out the 'accelerating present'. This is a step towards anticipating the *unknown unknowns*.

Illustration: Information supported decision-making - Beauty Time

Let's say we are making a decision about whether to open up a beauty treatment retail outlet - Beauty Time - in a *high street* in a medium-sized UK town.

First, check out data in the *public domain* that is readily available - data provided by the local authority on visitors to the high street.

Next, ideally we would like information on the number of people visiting the high street specifically looking for beauty care products.

However, it is unlikely that this is in the public domain; this will need a bespoke market research study. But this may be too costly.

So here why not spend one day of your own time in monitoring the number of people in the high street who go into shops in the beauty, health and wellbeing category. This footfall information could massively improve the quality of your decision about whether to and where to open a shop.

And to get some insights into the 'unknown unknowns' check out low cost or free industry reports on trends and developments in the beauty market.

The point being that a small investment of your time in collecting basic yet critical information will invariably substantially push up the probability of making a quality decision.

Balance the evidence and your intuition

We know that intuition – which can be described as knowing without knowing why – can be incredibly powerful. But it can also be a 'false friend'. At times applying so-called 'intuition' is just a lazy way of ignoring evidence and the facts. (The odds of winning the lottery with 1, 2, 3, 4, 5, 6 are the same as any other combination, but how many people will choose these?)

So it is critical to get the balance right between intuition and the evidence. This is why we have introduced the idea of 'informed intuition'.

This is about harnessing the power of System 1 (more emotional, intuitive and instinctive decision-making) whilst also utilising the rigor and discipline of System 2 (rational and analytical thinking).

Informed intuition in action

Let's take three examples of intuitive and creative thinking sitting alongside the hard evidence: Richard Branson, Steve Jobs and the Smart Car.

○ *Richard on the spot*

Richard Branson talks about decision-making as involving that 'little tingle', which is his term for the intuition that guides him towards his final decision.

But if we were to look at the process by which he chose the site for his first Virgin media store, we learn that his decision was not just driven by intuition.

Apparently he underpinned his instincts and intuition by conducting a market research study. He counted the number of people going into the different shop location options he was considering. So he had sound 'footfall data' on the different options to support his intuition.

○ *With a little help from market research*

Steve Jobs is well known for decrying the role of market research and customer opinion in developing new ideas. He believed that, if it was left to customers, they wouldn't have invented Apple. And no-one is denying the visionary status of Jobs.

However we now know that the Apple Corporation were regular commissioners of customer research studies to help validate and tweak Steve Jobs' initial inspirational ideas.

○ *That's Smart*

Mercedes made the decision not to provide a spare wheel in the Smart car because it would take up precious space that could be used for luggage.

This decision, in part, was inspired by creative thinking that challenged the status quo. If you can now use an aerosol to pump foam into the tyre as a temporary fix, why bother having a spare wheel at all? This was the insight. But interestingly, this creative decision was supported by some hard research data.

Market research studies showed that only a modest proportion of people knew how to change the wheel of a car. In addition only a small percentage had actually ever changed the wheel of a car by the side of the road. Moreover most people's go-to strategy in the event of a flat tyre would be to call a roadside breakdown service and/or a family member or friend to help them out.

This evidence reassured Mercedes that the announcement that there would be no spare wheel in the Smart car would *not* be greeted as anxious making, shock horror news. Their decision was grounded in innovative thinking, coupled with hard data about what motorists actually did, and how they felt about not having a spare wheel.

Be aware of the cognitive biases and influences in play

In arriving at informed decisions run your thinking past what we know about the cognitive biases and influences that are in play in many decision-making scenarios.

It was Knute Rockne who said, *'Most people, when they think they are thinking, are merely re-arranging their prejudices.'* So be familiar with the biases that might get in the way of informed decision-making.

Understanding how 'bias' affects decision-making is a big topic. But, to help, below we have outlined some – but not all – of the cognitive biases to be aware of in making an informed decision.

○ *Confirmation bias*: the decision-taker only focuses on information that confirms what they already think and want to believe.

○ *Familiarity bias*: The decision-taker is overly influenced by data, evidence and arguments with which they are familiar. Then they assign too greater a weight to this, thereby ignoring less familiar, but still very compelling data and arguments.

○ *Emotional investment bias:* When so much emotional energy has been invested in – sunk into – a venture, there is a reluctance to cancel a project or go in a different direction. You keep throwing good money after bad.

○ *The gambler's fallacy:* A belief that future probabilities are shaped by past events, whereas in fact they are not. We often think that 'lightening won't strike at the same place twice' but in fact it could.

○ *Optimism bias:* A tendency to overestimate the likelihood of good things happening to support the execution of a decision, whilst underestimating the probability of challenging events occurring.

○ *Halo bias:* Where the initial positive overall impression generated by say a new product reduces the willingness to accept that specific elements *within* this overall package still need attention.

A checklist of questions to help avoid the main decision-making minefields

Ask yourself the following questions to help ensure you are making an informed decision.

Am I denying that the challenge exists?

There is often a fundamental lack of awareness that a challenge or problem even exists. People often only see things as they want to see them, not as they really are. Some people switch off and are blind to certain issues. Thus, the start-point for sound decision-making is to ensure you are seeing it as it is.

Am I guilty of lazy, default and stereotypical thinking?

Much flawed decision-making stems from the fact that stakeholders have defaulted to working on the symptoms not the root cause of the problem. So remove any muddle or confusion around the core problem. Challenge received wisdom and call out any big underlying, but flawed, assumptions that could derail sound decision-making.

Am I failing to accept the facts?

Stakeholders often hold deeply entrenched positions based on long established beliefs. These create a prejudice against, and reluctance to accept, new incoming evidence. So be prepared to challenge entrenched positions.

Do I falsely believe that action has already been taken to address this issue?

People can come to believe that a problem has been solved simply because it has been identified. This is referred to as 'norming'. The classic illustration of this was the Challenger space shuttle disaster.

It was known that there could be a potential problem with a seal (O-ring) in the rocket engine at low temperature launching conditions. Thus, this problem and its consequences were recognised, but treated as 'normal' (solved) on the grounds that such low temperatures were very unlikely to occur.

This however was flawed reasoning. The problem – given its consequences – should have been fixed because tragically there were low temperatures on the day of the launch. The resulting explosion was an accident waiting to happen.

Am I being overly influenced by what the group around me are thinking?

Poor decisions may occur when stakeholders are overly influenced by what the wider decision-making group thinks.

To what extent is the framing of the problem influencing my objectivity?

If an idea is framed or introduced in a particular way, this '*priming*' could affect the likelihood of an informed decision being made.

A simple example would be someone framing evidence as: 'As <u>many</u> as 60% of customers were concerned about this'… as opposed to framing it as 'as <u>few</u> as 60% of customers…'

Am I reluctant to accept the evidence because it is too disruptive?

Another barrier to informed decision-making is the rejection of new evidence on the grounds it could lead to decisions that are organisationally disruptive and/or a personal hassle for the decision-makers.

Am I too frightened to make a U-turn and change my point of view?

People are often reluctant to do a sensible U-turn because they think this could be seen as a sign of weakness.

Am I guilty of using rules of thumb that are overly simplistic?

Decision-makers often apply simple intuitive heuristics they have always applied to understand their world, e.g. fast decision-making is always good decision-making. In some scenarios, this heuristic may apply, but in others it may <u>not</u>.

Am I zeroing in on the gains from making a decision rather than looking at the losses?

People think differently when an issue is couched in terms of the *losses* associated with a particular decision, as opposed to the decision being framed around the *gains* that could be achieved with this approach.

Am I using arbitrary rather than more rational decision criteria?

It is quite common for people to say 'let's go for a 50/50 solution' when there may be no logic to this particular split.

How accurate is my assessment of other people's likely reaction to my decision?

Some people have an exaggerated sense of the power and influence they can constructively exert over events once the decision is made.

Framing the decision options

To draw together the different lines of advice we have been offering about enhancing the quality of your thinking and decision-making readers may find the following framework helpful. It is a way of organising your thinking – a process to follow – when faced with a decision about which of several options to choose.

- *Frame* the different decision choices – options – that are available to you.

- For each of the decision options you have framed, identify the *opportunities* this opens up.

- Then identify the *risks* associated with each option.

- Now assess the *likelihood of success* of each option.

- Then look at the *consequences* of pursuing each decision option.

You're now in a position to weigh up all the evidence, the pros and cons, of each of the decision options to arrive at your *final decision*.

Getting your decisions actioned

Once a problem has been identified and a decision made, there still remains the challenge of ensuring the appropriate action is actually taken to deliver what has been decided. Often an issue is identified but then not linked to a concrete process for taking action to solve – remove – the problem.

Problem *resolving* requires three steps:

- First, clearly *crystallising* the *problem* in a few succinct sentences.

- Next, mapping out the *consequences* of not addressing this problem in an effective and timely way.

- Then following through to identify the *precise action* needed to satisfactorily deal with this challenge.

Let's take a look at a hotel example of the problem resolution process in action.

Illustration: A hotel example of effective problem resolution

There's a problem with water leaking onto the floor of the washroom in a hotel's main reception area.

A loose management approach to resolving this problem would involve noting this in some form of log – putting it on a 'things to do' list and hoping it gets sorted sooner rather than later.

In contrast, a systematic approach to problem resolution leads to remedial action that means things start to happen. This would involve the following:

- **Crystallise the problem:** precisely define the problem: 'There is a leak from the X pipe which is creating puddles on a large surface area of the reception washroom.'

- **Articulate the consequences:** This could mean 'a guest slipping and seriously injuring themselves resulting in an expensive lawsuit and/or a guest falling and damaging their clothing resulting in adverse social media posts that will be to the detriment of the hotel.'

- **Decide on and specify the practical action to be taken:** This could be something like 'to reduce risk, effective remedial action must be taken by a designated staff member within *five minutes* of the incident being reported.'

You get the idea. It's moving away from the 'passive' observation of a challenge accompanied by vague and woolly suggestions for resolving this problem towards a more assertive approach. This is one whereby clear informed decisions on the optimum way of resolving this problem are tightly linked to an 'effective problem resolution process' that ensures the decision – resolution – will be implemented.

Be a critical thinker

To sum up our guide to effective decision-making we now provide some general principles about being a critical thinker.

Be open-minded

A key dimension to critical thinking is the ability to examine an issue from different perspectives. Spinoza said, *'No matter how thin you slice it, there will always be two sides.'* And F. Scott Fitzgerald wrote *'The test of a first-rate intelligence is the ability to hold two opposed ideas in mind at the same time, and still retain the ability to function.'*

This sounds simple enough doesn't it but putting it in to practice can be tricky. For example, if you are passionate about allowing animals to live in the wild, not in captivity, you might <u>not</u> welcome evidence to show that certain species would just not have survived without the intervention of those running zoos (apparently this is true of the Micronesian kingfisher – a story you might want to check out.)

Stay curious

When you see a statistic or an observation being made, just how motivated are you to check out its veracity. Do you just accept this or immediately go for the fact checker.

For example, if you saw a stat that told you only 2% of shoes sold in the United States are actually made in the USA, do you just take this in your stride and accept it?

Or do you start asking some questions? How come a major industrialised country doesn't have a bigger shoe industry? Surely, with all those cows roaming around Texas, there must be loads of leather to form the basis for such an industry and so on.

Well, apparently, it is true. 98% of shoes sold in the United States are imported! But it is a standout stat that needs checking rather than instantly being accepted.

Apply 'self-monitoring'

We are using the term self-monitoring to refer to always asking yourself whether you *really* understand an issue in sufficient depth before taking a decision. And if not, are you then prepared to improve your current depth of understanding before coming to a judgement. Let's provide a quick example to illustrate this point.

Let's say someone tells you that when you put an ice cube into warm water the ice cube cools down the water. Do you accept this given that it sounds reasonably plausible? Or do you go further with your thinking?

If you do go further you will learn that it is a bit more complicated than this. Apparently when we put ice in water, the ice doesn't just give its cold to the water. It also takes heat from the water. And the full explanation doesn't stop here. This would take us into the dynamics of heat transfer (which then gets a bit too complicated for me!)

Here the central point we are making is how motivated are you to keep questioning yourself about whether you feel you have got a sufficiently in-depth understanding of how something *really works*.

So in summary, the critical thinker will develop the skill of always trying to understand the wider context. They will work hard at asking ever-more powerful and penetrating questions to get to the heart of an issue. They will be fascinated by what causes an issue – occurrences and events – and enjoy working through the likely effects and consequences. They will *enjoy* thinking. They won't see it as a chore.

Invest in improving your decision-making skills

The idea of encouraging someone to make informed decisions seems trite – why would anyone want to make an uninformed decisions?

What seems to have happened in the world of entrepreneurialism is that intuition, which nobody is denying is incredibly powerful, has been put centre stage. But this tends to downplay the importance of setting intuition alongside the available evidence.

So this is why we are driving home the importance of applying the concept of 'informed intuition'. This is about getting the right balance in your decision-making between using intuition and respecting the hard evidence.

Key actions

✓ Learn to enjoy critical thinking – make sure you carve out time and space to do your decision-making justice.

✓ Make sure you're always working on the right problem and have clarity around the 'problem you're solving for'. Understand all of the underlying assumptions that have gone into the way the problem was first presented.

✓ Make sure you hit the sweet spot between using the power of intuition and entrepreneurial flair. But temper this with understanding the facts and realities. Go for 'informed intuition'.

→ *Carve out time and space for clear deep thinking. Smart thinking is a critical part of the entrepreneur's job.*

20: MASTER WINNING WAYS
Highlights

Win the inner game

Think of cultivating the **Entrepreneur Mindset** as being a game you must win. Victory will provide the platform for ensuring that disruptive behaviours don't throw you off course.

Takes ownership for problems, make things happen and drive action. **Make critical and timely interventions** rather than just letting things drift in the vague hope they will improve.

It's worth investing time in **building effective self-management strategies** and techniques that you can apply to different business challenges.

Be the best version of yourself

Winning entrepreneurs show up with lots of **presence** - bags of physical and forensic energy.

Cultivate winning habits - create the 'winner's advantage' and avoid the 'loser's curse'. **Make your own luck.**

Know what makes up **the winner's mindset**. What are the attitudes and behaviours you must bring to the party to make an entrepreneurial impact?

Honour the struggle

Develop coping strategies to handle the highs and lows of what can be a roller-coaster entrepreneurial journey.

There will be times where you need to **raise your game** - honour the struggle and take action - even when this is stressful and does not come naturally.

Build the self-awareness and control required to **turn on your A-Game** at will and create winning outcomes. Remember if you are working for yourself, it is always your fault!

THE WINNER'S FORMULA: Passion and persistence

Master winning ways

How dare you settle for less when the world has made it so easy for you to be remarkable.
Seth Godin

The entrepreneurial journey is exciting but can be demanding. So you need to cultivate coping strategies and techniques that will build your resilience and enable you to deal with challenges and barriers that may stand in your way.

It is about mastering 'winning ways' – acquiring the winner's mindset. And at the heart of a winning mindset is building the 'capability' to deal with challenging situations. And here we would define capability as 'self-trust in one's ability to figure out what action must be taken to achieve a desired outcome.'

Manage your thoughts: foster winning ways

Take ownership and strive for consistent excellence

Be resilient and tenacious

Recognise that it's always down to you

The tough reality for entrepreneurs is the need to accept that it is always your fault!

Winning entrepreneurs always take ownership for problems and make critical interventions rather than letting things drift in the vague hope that things will resolve themselves.

You will need to be the person who is on it 24/7 constantly scanning the horizon, being prepared to take action on different fronts in order to deliver your vision and goals.

One way to think of your role is as a 'linchpin' who Seth Godin defines as *'An individual who can walk into chaos and create order. Someone who can invent, connect, create and make things happen.'*

And our message throughout this book is that you can become the person with these 'linchpin' qualities if you work at cultivating the Entrepreneur Mindset.

Commit to excellence

As a self-employed entrepreneur you need to take personal responsibility for improving your skillset. Develop an obsession with improving key capabilities that will take you in the direction of your goals. Commit to constantly improving your skills and striving towards excellence.

Studies on high performance show that a commitment to mastering critical skills is a key to success. Malcolm Gladwell tells us that the hallmark of many successful people is that they put in that 10,000 hours of persistent effort to hone their skills. It's about creating that 'competence confidence virtuous circle' we referred to earlier. Gary Player, the golfer, said *'The more I practice the luckier I get.'*

Be a consistent high performer

In business, as in sport, the difference between being an average performer and a champion is *consistent* excellence. This is why successful entrepreneurs not only strive to achieve high standards of excellence, but also learn how to do this on a regular basis.

It's no good being an amateur, dilettante or dabbler who only occasionally brings their A-Game to the party – it's about consistency.

Thus, if confidence begins to wain and self-doubt and limiting beliefs begin to kick in, you need to have – as we introduced earlier – 'triggers' to remind yourself to switch out of negative thinking mode into a more positive outcome mindset.

Set up success triggers

Identify success 'triggers' that will ensure that key entrepreneurial traits become routine and eventually habits.

Examples of simple triggers to help build habits

So why not leave your trainers out in the evening to remind you to go on an early morning run and meet your 10,000 steps target.

Put the TV remote away in a drawer to remind you to limit your TV consumption.

When on a business Zoom call – put on your 'Zoom' shirt to remind you to turn up in *'showtime'* mode.

Keep a journal

A journal is a great way of making sure you cultivate the habits of the high performance entrepreneur. With a journal you can document the triggers to high performance that work best for you.

A journal will allow you to monitor your progress and see where you are making great strides forward, and where there may have been shortfalls you can correct.

Cultivating the winner's advantage

Some principles to help cultivate the winner's advantage and avoid the loser's curse include:

- Ensure you have total clarity over what it is you want to achieve. This crystallisation will start tilting the odds in your favour.

- Acknowledge that you cannot do everything but believe that if you can't do something you will find a way of figuring it out. Hard work puts you where luck can find you.

- Focus on each task in hand and act with purpose and intentionality to achieve a successful outcome.

- Visualise success: in this way you're more likely to make things happen for you.

- Constantly be anticipating what might happen next. Luck happens when preparation meets opportunity.

○ When things do not go your way, learn from this. Identify where there were uncontrollables that you couldn't do anything about. But be honest in pinpointing shortfalls in your own performance that provide you with lessons about how to improve going forward.

○ Be lucky: Accept that there is a slightly woo-woo element to cultivating the 'winners' advantage'. It was Napoleon, when asked what he's looking for in a General, who replied, *'They need to be lucky.'* And it was WH Murray, the Scottish explorer, who said, *'The moment one definitely commits oneself then providence moves too.'* This is slightly mystical, but in essence this is saying that if you apply the above principles then you will attract success – you will find that that the universe will conspire in your favour.

Be resilient and tenacious

Entrepreneurs who know how to win recognise the need to *honour the struggle*. The high performance entrepreneur is *tenacious* and is persistent in making things happen. They will do things that need doing in a timely way even when they do not feel like doing them.

Albert Einstein said, *'It's not that I'm so smart, it's just that I stay with problems longer.'* So winning entrepreneurs are prepared to follow through on their actions and persevere even in the face of initial adversity. They show single-minded determination.

You need to be courageous

High performers develop the mental strength – the *courage* – to push boundaries and challenge conventional wisdom. TS Eliot said, *'Only those who will risk going too far can possibly find out how far one can go.'*

Winning entrepreneurs stay true to their cause and not let crazy-makers and doubters undercut their efforts to deliver outstanding high performance.

They will resist negative forces that are pulling them away from delivering the best possible outcome. They will not be deflected from their goals.

There is an awareness that on their entrepreneurial journey there will be battles ahead that will need to be fought, but they have the courage to address these.

Operate with integrity

In this chapter we have been promoting the idea of being a winner. But this is not about winning at any cost. It is about doing this with integrity.

The Four Agreements

When it comes to operating with integrity a wonderful set of guiding principles are the *Four Agreements* from Don Miguel Ruiz.

First, *Be impeccable with your word* (be honest and show integrity).

Second, *Don't take anything personally* (accept there is usually two sides to every issue).

Third, *Don't make assumptions* (assess all the evidence before you leap to any kind of conclusion).

Fourth, *Always do your best* (in the moment).

I'm OK/You're OK

The classic *I'm OK/You're OK* framework model is another guide to achieving outcomes with integrity – and respecting the other person.

It is often easy to find a one-sided win (*I'm OK* but the other person is *Not OK*).

Similarly, it is easy to give in to a situation where you are *Not OK,* but the other person *Is OK*.

Your goal should be to arrive at the *I'm OK/You're OK* sweet spot – demonstrating sensitivity and empathy with the other person's position, but still ensuring you achieve your purpose.

Be a winner not a victim

The theme running through this chapter – and indeed the entire book - is that it is possible to cultivate a winning Entrepreneur Mindset. The traits that make up a person who knows how to make ideas happen are not a given – they can be nurtured. There are thought processes you can manage to achieve this.

The key point here is that 'thoughts' are just that: they are not necessarily grounded in reality. They are things that come across your mind that can be 'processed'. You can think yourself into the winning mindset. It is possible by following the principles and techniques in this book to put yourself on the right side of good fortune. And not give up at the first sign of failure.

Confident entrepreneurs with the winning mindset *do not* have superpowers. And if they do, it is simply the confidence that comes from knowing that if they cannot do something they will (eventually) always be able to figure it out.

So in building the winner's mindset, there is the need to commit to excellence and put in the time to acquire the necessary knowledge, skills and competence. This will build your confidence. In this way you will find that things will start conspiring in your favour, rather than against you. This mixture of belief, being centred and taking action only works!

Key actions

✓ Take personal responsibility for sorting out what needs fixing.

✓ Make sure you're gradually becoming better and better at the key skills you need for success.

✓ Tenaciously follow through to ensure that ideas become actions then successful outcomes.

→ *Always show up with your A-Game: with bags of physical and forensic energy.*

21: CULTIVATE SUCCESS HABITS

In the final chapter of the book we summarise the seven key dimensions of the Entrepreneur Mindset with the aim of encouraging you to make sure these success habits become engrained into your psyche – things you do naturally. These are:

Set your **Direction** of travel

Cultivate mental **Resilience**

Take decisive **Action**

Apply clear **Thinking**

Be **Different**

Be **Influential**

Deliver consistent **High Performance**

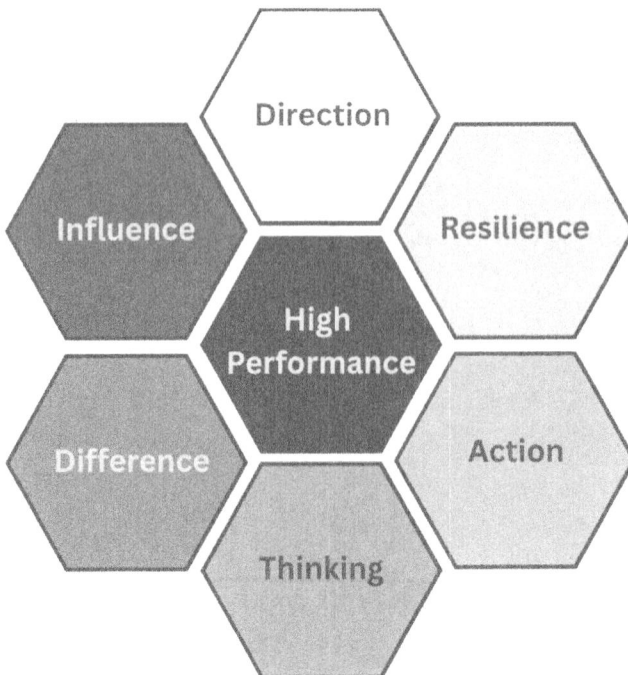

Cultivate success habits

We are what we repeatedly do. Excellence then is not an act but a habit.

Aristotle

In this concluding chapter, we review each dimension of the Entrepreneur Mindset. As you read each summary why not identify ways in which you can turn these into success habits by setting up *triggers* to prompt you to consistently follow best practice. In this way you build up habits that become engrained in your muscle memory.

But your choice of specific triggers must be your own personal decision. This is not something we can prescribe for you – it will depend on your personality and situation.

Direction: Set your Direction

We started by emphasising the need to get total clarity around what it is you want to achieve – your direction of travel. This is the starting point for your entrepreneurial journey.

Entrepreneurial success begins with having an inspirational **Vision** of what you want to achieve – one that is authentic and reflects the kind of person you are and the business you want to build.

We explained that this vision is the platform for setting specific **Goals** and that it is good practice to write these down and monitor on a regular basis.

We then focused on always acting with **Purpose** and intentionality to deliver your vision and achieve your goals.

Resilience: Cultivate Mental Resilience

Next we stressed the need for mental strength, having the resilience needed to deal with the highs and lows on the entrepreneurial journey.

We looked at building positive **Beliefs**. Ensure there aren't any nagging limiting or destructive beliefs that will block your entrepreneurial journey. Call out and tackle any limiting beliefs that are holding you back and sabotaging your entrepreneurial potential. It is about taking ownership – being a leader, not a follower and cultivating mental resilience.

It's also about building a healthy relationship with money. Think **Abundance** and showcase the value you provide (and should be rewarded for). Here, a powerful way to build mental strength is to 'reframe' any belief that is blocking you: delete that negative programme – and then replace it with a positive version. Do this regularly as a ritual and it will help you consistently operate with a strong mindset.

We then addressed the need to **Overcome adversity**. Accept that things rarely go according to plan first time out of the box. Acknowledge that you need to take personal responsibility for figuring out and fixing things. Be tenacious in driving things through.

Action: Take Decisive Action

As an entrepreneur, you must take massive decisive action.

We highlighted the power of thinking yourself into a high **Energy** register – one which fosters powerful forensic thinking.

We then focused on what taking **Action** entails. This is about always avoiding procrastination, getting projects underway and not worrying at the beginning too much about the 'how'. It is about learning as you go.

Then we turned to being **Super productive**. This is about protecting your time, and focusing on what matters most. Get a big win in the bag early in the day before the day's distractions begin to take their toll. Make this way of working a morning ritual.

Specifically we recommended the 90 minute 'block time' practice: begin each day with a major 'big rock' activity that will deliver a key outcome. With this achieved, you can then tackle the other tasks and activities on your plate.

Thinking: Apply Clear Thinking

The next dimension – habit of the successful entrepreneur – is to always apply clear thinking to every decision.

This clear thinking is critical to achieving **Strategic excellence:** operating from a position of strength. You must play where you are most likely to win and create a differentiated offer that provides your customers with the emotional benefits they are seeking.

We then examined the idea of providing creative **Simple solutions**. Remove confusion and noise from what you are doing. Set up an effortless operation with a product and/or service that is intuitive and easy to use for customers.

Many entrepreneurs get so carried away with their idea that they do not first ensure it is grounded in a sound business model. So we spelt out the payoff of applying **Business acumen** to everything you do.

Difference: Be Different

We then highlighted the necessity, as an entrepreneur in a crowded and competitive marketplace, to be different.

We highlighted that today **Creativity** is increasingly a major differentiator and stressed how everyone's creativity can be taken to the next level by self-belief and applying simple creativity techniques.

We looked at how an in-depth understanding of your customers and stakeholders – knowing how to **Touch their world** – is a major source of differentiation. It's about making sure you deliver memorable, transformational experiences that will be treasured by customers and shared with others.

And then we identified the need to have confidence to **Showcase your difference**. Create a succinct Elevator Pitch and brand message that elegantly conveys to the marketplace and stakeholders why you are different.

Influence: Be Influential

The Entrepreneur Mindset embraces being influential. We explained that it was unhelpful to think of influence as being some kind of manipulation. Think of being influential as helping people see different perspectives.

In setting up your own personal or company brand, we stressed that your brand is a set of promises you are making. Ensure your branding is **Authentic** – it is a reflection of you.

We hit home that marketing what you do is almost more important than doing what you do and examined the art of **Telling your story** as a powerful way of extending your influence and authority.

Stories tap into people's emotions and take customers and stakeholders on a journey that they will enjoy listening to.

We then turned to ensuring your brand stays **Relevant**. Constantly adapt to change. Keep your antenna up. Ensure you have a panorama view of what is going on in your industry. Take action if you see anything on the horizon that needs addressing.

High Performance: Deliver High Performance

In the final part of the book we looked at high performance – always consistently showing up with your A-Game.

We made the case for **Informed decision-making**. We introduced the idea of 'informed intuition', getting the right balance between System 1 (more emotion- based) thinking and System 2 (more evidence-based) thinking.

Then we focused on mastering **Winning ways:** turning the odds in your favour – making your own luck. It is about cultivating the winner's mindset: it's about anticipating events, taking ownership and always showing up – being there to sort things out.

And our book culminated with the idea of **Cultivating success habits**. It's about turning the seven dimensions of the Entrepreneur Mindset into habits that become engrained into how you seize each day.

So we have now reached a point where it is simply a matter of you believing, being bold, and taking action to make your own ideas happen.

'Whatever you think you can do or believe you can do, begin it. Action has magic, grace and power in it.'

Goethe

I hope you have found this book – your practical guide to building the Entrepreneur Mindset – helpful. Every success with your own entrepreneurial journey.

NOTES

Introduction

The aim of this book has been to provide *practical* actions you can take to cultivate the **Entrepreneur Mindset** and develop the art of making ideas happen. Therefore we have not burdened the reader with a detailed follow-up reading list.

However, we recognise that some readers may want to explore further some of the key principles we have outlined in this book.

Therefore, for each Part, we have selected *three references* that provide a starter for delving into this dimension of the Entrepreneur Mindset.

Part One: Set Your Direction

In this Part of the book we focused on shaping your vision, setting motivational goals and focusing with purpose. To reinforce these principles for those who want to read further, we have selected a book by Seth Godin entitled *'The Icarus Deception'*. Aspiring entrepreneurs should find this inspirational because it talks about moving away from the old idea of playing it safe – staying within your comfort zone – and not flying too close to the sun. It entreats us to develop a vision and have the guts to do something about it.

The second book selected is *'Opportunity'* by Eben Pagan. He is an outstanding US entrepreneur whose CV includes being a rock guitarist, coppersmith apprentice, real estate agent and dating guru. He is now a leading expert on entrepreneurship. There is lots of great advice in this book about seizing opportunities in a timely way.

And finally, we recommend that you check the UK *Dragon's Den* TV programme, where you can compare and contrast what makes for successful, as opposed to less well-thought-through, entrepreneurial ventures.

So together these three recommendations should provide some inspiration and lots of food for thought in building and sustaining your vision and direction of travel.

Part Two: Cultivate Mental Resilience

Here, we looked at building positive beliefs, operating in abundance, not scarcity, mode and building the skills and mindset to overcome adversity.

At the heart of the message in this part of the book is the notion of learning how to manage your thoughts. Thus the first book we recommend is Michael Neill's *'The Inside-Out Revolution'*. He is an authority on constructively managing thought processes and building positive beliefs.

On the theme of understanding and managing emotions and thoughts, we are also recommending *'The Chimp Paradox: The mind management programme for confidence, success and happiness'*, by Dr Steve Peters. He has been a coach to many top Olympic athletes and sports people.

And finally we would suggest checking out *'Mindset: Changing the way you think to fulfil your potential'*, by Dr Carol S. Dweck. This will focus you on developing the growth not fixed mindset which is a key part of entrepreneurial success.

Part Three: Take Decisive Action

In this Part of the book we examined the importance of ensuring you manage your energy levels and build the critical habit of always taking action, and then being super productive, including managing the most precious commodity of all – your time.

Here we are recommending is *'Hyperfocus: How to work less and achieve more'*, by Chris Bailey.

Then, given the importance of entrepreneurs operating in an agile, focused way, we suggest you look **at** *'Scrum: The art of doing twice the work in half the time'*, by Jeff Sutherland.

A further recommendation to check out is *'Building a Second Brain: A proven method to organize your digital life and unlock your creative potential'*, by Tiago Forte. You will get lots of ideas on how to cope with all the information that is coming across your desk, make sense of it and take action in a productive way.

Four: Apply Clear Thinking

The spotlight here was on applying clear strategic thinking to everything you do, providing simple solutions, and always operating with clarity when monetising your entrepreneurial idea.

On the theme of improving critical thinking and making astute strategic decisions, check out *'Seeing What Others Don't: The remarkable ways we gain insights'*, by Gary Klein.

Here, as a start point for enhancing your problem solving skills, we would recommend *'Pig Wrestling: The brilliantly simple way to solve any problem... and create the change you need'*, by Pete Lindsay and Mark Bawden.

To reinforce the power of the minimum viable product approach to getting a business venture underway, we would suggest *'The Lean Startup: How constant innovation creates radically successful businesses'*, by Eric Ries.

Part Five: Be Different

In this Part of the book we highlighted the value of always adding a creative edge to everything you do as an entrepreneur.

We looked at touching your customer's world by demonstrating your depth of understanding of their needs and requirements. And we also stressed the need for confidence in creatively showcasing why you are different.

Here we recommend that you look at Julia Cameron's international best seller *'The Artist's Way: A course in discovering and recovering your creative self'*.

And, you will get lots of creative inspiration from *'Alchemy: The surprising power of ideas that don't make sense'*, by Rory Sutherland.

And when it comes to creating a difference, based on an in-depth understanding of human behaviour, there are lots of lessons in *'The Moment of Clarity: Using the human sciences to solve your toughest business problems'*, by Madsbjerg and Rasmussen.

Part Six: Be Influential

We introduced the idea of you becoming a brand and the importance of your brand authentically representing who you are as a person. We also looked at bringing your entrepreneurial journey alive as a compelling story that will establish your credentials in the marketplace. We then addressed the issue of keeping your brand relevant and up-to-date.

A start point is to look at *'The Art of Influence: Persuading others begins with you'*, by Chris Widener. We selected this because it drives home the importance of ensuring that integrity and authenticity is the golden thread that runs through all your communications.

To better understand how great presenters such as Steve Jobs went about their business, why not look at *'The Presentation Secrets of Steve Jobs: How to be insanely great in front of any audience'*, by Carmine Gallo.

And finally we would suggest you look at Part Two of the DVL Smith book *'The High Performance Customer Insight Professional'*. This is because it provides a number of story structures that you can use as templates for helping construct impactful business communications.

Part Seven: Deliver High Performance

In the final Part of the book we examined the art of making informed judgements and decisions, reviewed the power of acquiring winning ways, and stressed the importance of cultivating success habits.

On the subject of decision-making, we suggest you look at *'Nudge'*, by Richard H Thaler and Cass R Sunstein, as a reminder of the need to understand the key cognitive biases that shape how we all make decisions.

We also suggest that you dip into *'The Winning Mindset: What sport can teach us about great leadership'*, by Damian Hughes. This has some great stories and lessons on delivering high performance under pressure.

And finally we would recommend looking at *'High Performance Habits: How extraordinary people become that way'*. This is an authoritative publication by the inspirational US performance coach Brendon Burchard.

Once again, every success with your entrepreneurial adventure.

ACKNOWLEDGMENTS

I'd like to thank Jo Smith for her outstanding contribution to the creation of this book. Jo has been a long standing Director of DVL Smith Ltd with responsibilities for finance, IT, people and office management. These wide ranging roles have given her a keen eye on what it takes to build, with integrity, a successful business. Her judgement and advice on what principles and techniques to share in this book with those who want to embark on the entrepreneurial way of life has been invaluable.

Thanks also to Anne Scott for editing the text and taking full responsibility for the design, layout and formatting of the book. A considerable amount of expertise, professionalism and experience went into ensuring that this book reached the high standards required in the field of publishing.

I would also like to thank Alexia Smith for preparing different drafts of the book. This required considerable dedication and patience.

And finally, thanks to Calla Scott for her work on the cover of the book.

The Entrepreneur Mindset

I hope you enjoyed reading this book and applying the techniques we have outlined to make your ideas happen.

DVL Smith offers a range of consultancy and coaching services for entrepreneurs; we would be delighted to talk to you further about building your **Entrepreneur Mindset**.

Contact:

david.smith@dvlsmith.com

dvlsmith.com

Printed in Great Britain
by Amazon